The Complete Indian Cookbook

The Complete Indian Cookbook

TIGER BOOKS INTERNATIONAL
LONDON

A QUINTET BOOK

This edition published in 1992
by Tiger Books International PLC, London

ISBN 1-85501-288-X

This book was designed and produced by
Quintet Publishing Limited
6 Blundell Street
London N7 9BH

Designer: Nicky Chapman
Editor: Diana Vowles

Material in this book previously appeared in *Indian
Regional Cooking, Step-by-Step Indian Cooking* and
Indian Vegetarian Cooking

Typeset in Great Britain by
Central Southern Typesetters, Eastbourne
Manufactured in Singapore by
Eray Scan Pte Ltd
Printed in Singapore by
Star Standard Industries Pte Ltd

Contents

Above The palm groves of Kerala in
southern India provide plenty of
coconuts, an essential ingredient of
many local dishes.

Introduction

. . . .

India is a land of spectacular contrasts, from the emerald Vale of Kashmir in the snow-clad mountains of the north to the steaming jungles and palm-fringed beaches of the tropical south. Across this vast country of 700 million inhabitants the intricate use of spices unites all the kitchens of the land into producing food that is uniquely Indian. There are about 25 spices on the shelf in the Indian pantry. Many of them will have come from the back garden along with fresh herbs and bulbs – onions, garlic and shallots. With this huge treasury of flavours the Indian cook can create an infinite number of different dishes. Spices can be used individually or combined, roasted or ground with water into a paste to produce flavours anywhere in the spectrum from sweet to sour, fiery to bland and fragrant to pungent.

Indians are almost intuitively aware of the medicinal properties of the herbs and spices they use to flavour their food, and they eat not just for sheer enjoyment and to stay alive, but to keep their bodies healthy and well-tuned. Apart from their medicinal properties, spices and other condiments can be used to offset the extremes of temperature. In the north, warming spices take the bite out of freezing winter days, and in the south bitter-sweet tamarind has a soothing effect in the airless midday heat.

Of course what is eaten also depends largely on local produce. Broadly speaking, bread is eaten in the north and rice in the south. In the south the food tends to be more fiery (and paradoxically more refreshing, even if it does bring tears to the eyes). In Kerala, in particular, grow the coconut palms, the tamarind and jackfruit trees and the spice gardens that made Cochin rich and famous.

In the south, the tropical heat is put to use to mature pickles and for overnight fermentation of bread and cakes made from ground peas without the addition of yeast. Southerners often steam their food, whereas in the north it is oven-cooked. In Rajasthan in the northwest, picnickers make an impromptu oven by digging a pit for a cow-dung fire on which they will cook spiced meat in a clay pot. The lid of the pot is sealed with dough, and more burning dung is heaped over it. This technique is called "dum" – food is baked slowly all the way through and all the juices are kept in, resulting in the tenderest meat and the richest possible flavour.

In Kashmir the winters are made bearable by cooking with warming spices, particularly cinnamon. People carry around baskets of live charcoal to keep the cold at bay between meals, and these baskets serve a double purpose, often baking an egg or a potato for a hot snack.

Kashmir is a land of lakes and tranquil water gardens. The lakes produce abundant fish and delicious lotus roots. Ingenious farmers make floating vegetable gardens from reeds and mud, which can be towed about or left to drift picturesquely at anchor. When they are harvested, vegetables are sold from boats at the floating market. As autumn draws in there is a frenzy of mushroom picking and all kinds of vegetables, especially chillies, are hung up on the rafters to dry to keep the family supplied when the snows come. To see them through

Opposite and left From the exuberance of the Palace of the Four Winds at Jaipur to the simplicity of the local post office, India is a sub-continent with many architectural delights.

Above For most of the time the elephant is a humble beast of burden, earning its keep by carrying and pulling heavy loads, but on festive occasions is profusely decorated and becomes the centre of much attention.

the winter, the Kashmiris make a dried spice cake called *ver*, crushing their spices according to a family recipe, then mixing them to a paste with mustard oil. The cake is hung up and bits are broken off it as required.

In the east, the Bengalis are noted for their love of fish and their insatiable desire for sweets, especially jaggery (raw sugar). Sugar cane is pressed to extract the juice, which is then heated over wood fires and patiently stirred for many hours until it is thick enough to set. Lumps of it are eaten as sweets and the Bengalis are so fond of it that they even manage to slip it into their vegetable curries.

Bombay in Maharashtra on the west coast, India's Hollywood and boom town founded on seven islands, has its own sweet treats –

biscuits made of rice flour. They take several days and many processes to make, and are served at religious festivals.

Lucknow in Uttar Pradesh glories in whole chickens stuffed with quails, and a celebration halva made from the yolks of 100 eggs. Another local extravagance is a pearl pilaf – a dish of rice and "pearls" made by stuffing a chicken's oesophagus with a mixture of egg yolks and real gold and silver, and tying it at intervals to resemble a string of pearls. It is then boiled and slit open, and the "pearls" pop out, looking very like the real thing.

All over India, the laws of religion rule what is eaten. Hindus are vegetarian, although the priestly caste of Kashmiri Brahmins do eat meat, abstaining instead

from cooking with garlic and onions, which they believe inflame the passions. Jains are such strict vegetarians that they will neither eat root vegetables, for fear of killing insects as they dig, nor will they touch tomatoes or aubergines, whose colour reminds them of blood. The Muslims will not eat pork and nowhere except in the state of Kerala is it permitted to kill the sacred cow. One sect of Muslims, the Bohris, alternate salt and sweet dishes and begin their meal by eating a pinch of salt in praise of Allah.

Presenting the meal

The traditional way to serve Indian food is on a thali or large tray, often of beautiful wrought metal. Each different dish will be in a small metal or earthenware bowl perched around the edge of the tray, or laid out on a low communal brass table. The diners sit on the floor, or on very low stools. The carpet is spread with coloured cloth to protect it and the guests are given giant coloured napkins. The dishes can be wrapped in cotton or silk, which is loosely folded back over the food after it has been served. Often banana leaves will serve as disposable plates. More people today are sitting up to a table with chairs, although in many parts the men are still served first, and then the women eat together on the floor in the kitchen.

Indians eat with their hands. The right hand only is used – the left is thought unclean. In some parts of India the whole hand is used; in others just the fingertips. Generally, food is scooped up with a piece of flat bread in the north and mopped up with rice in the south. It means that cleanliness is very important – hands are washed before and after eating and water for washing is provided even on barrows selling snacks in the streets.

In all parts of India hospitality is legendary. All the dishes, including fruit and sweetmeats, are offered at once. Decoration is simple (nuts, chopped herbs, lemon slices) and sometimes exotic – silver and gold leaf *vark* on special occasions provide a direct, although expensive, source of minerals.

Above Nuts are used in both savoury and sweet Indian recipes. This nut vendor is a well-known figure outside the Amber Palace in Rajasthan.

Cold water is drunk with meals. Breakfast, which might be a sweet flaky bread in the foothills of the Himalayas, a potato curry in the capital, Delhi, or a steamed bean cake (idli) in the south, is served with tea, sometimes spiced with cinnamon, or with hot strong coffee. During the day an Indian might drink freshly pressed fruit juice (mango is the favourite), coconut milk (in the south), or lassi, a sweet and sometimes salty drink made from yoghurt. Muslims are forbidden alcohol, but there is plenty of potent liquor about for whose who want it. Other drinks include Asha, which is distilled from jaggery, palm toddy and, of course, gin.

After a meal the hostess may offer betel leaves – glossy green leaves with mildly anaesthetic properties and a refreshing taste. These are chewed and then spat out (or more delicately removed), like gum. They can be taken neat or wrapped around nuts, quicklime, cardamon pods, cloves or tobacco. Shah Jahan, one of Indian's more colourful rulers and the builder of the Taj Mahal as a mausoleum for his wife Mumtaz, was even known to wrap them around poison for his less-welcome guests.

This book offers enticing meat dishes from the north; from the east, characteristic fish delicacies. The vegetable dishes originate mainly in the south and west. From the south, too, come coconut, hot spicy vegetable dishes and lentils. This is a comprehensive collection of recipes: the flavour is wholly Indian.

Top Indians are intuitively aware of the medicinal properties of certain foods and the medicine man's stall will often display herbs and spices also available from food stalls.

Bottom Sweet stalls are a common sight in the streets of Indian cities, particularly in western regions. Made from liquid sugar, many varieties are too sweet for the Western palate.

Spices and aromatics in the Indian kitchen

Spices and aromatics are the very heart of Indian cooking. Flowers, leaves, roots, bark, seeds and bulbs (the simplest of natural ingredients) are used in endless combinations to produce an infinite variety of flavours: sweet, sharp, hot, sour, spicy, aromatic, tart, mild, fragrant or pungent.

The Indian cook aims to create blends of spices so subtle that a completely new taste arises – something indefinable. Sometimes the flavour of one particular spice can be magnified by the careful underplay of several others. As many as 15 spices may be used in one dish, or there might be only one. Spices, unlike herbs, can be used together without loss of flavour.

It is best to buy your spices whole and to grind them at home (see page 25) if the recipe calls for it. Whole spices keep longer than spice powders, which quickly lose their aroma. But even whole spices begin to taste tired after a while so buy small quantities and keep them in airtight jars in a cool dark place. Do not buy curry powder – this is a blanket term for a blend of inferior spices which will make everything taste the same.

Asafoetida (*Hing*)
This is a resin and comes from Kashmir. It is bought ground and is said to smell of truffles. The flavour is quite pungent, but it is used mainly for its digestive properties, especially in the cooking of beans, where it combats flatulence. A pinch of it can be fried in hot oil before the rest of the ingredients are cooked.

Biriyani masala
This is a special sweet spice mix for biriyani dishes. Grind together the cardamom seeds from 8 pods, 25 g/ 1 oz cinnamon stick, 6 cloves and 1 tsp fennel seeds.

Cardamom (*Elaichi*)
Pale green cardamom pods contain tiny black seeds and grow in the rain forests of southern India. They have a sweet fragrant flavour and can be used whole (although the pod is not usually eaten) or the seeds can be taken out of the pods and used separately. This is a fiddly business, but seeds are not usually sold out of their pods because they lose their flavour too fast. Some recipes use ground cardamom seeds and as they are so small, it is best to grind them with a pestle and mortar.

Cayenne pepper (*Pisi hui lal mirch*)
Cayenne pepper, like paprika, comes from the seeds of plants in the capsicum family. It is a blend of various types of chilli powder. The capsicum family is large, ranging from the sweet pepper to the chilli. In general, the smaller the fruit, the hotter it is. Cayenne is sold as a powder. It should not be as hot as chilli powder, but it is pretty hot and should therefore be used with care.

Chilli (*Mirchi*)
Chilli is the hottest flavour on earth. Chillies and chilli powder should be used with extreme care. Do not take a bite of a chilli or even lick one to see how it tastes as the effect will be quite devastating. Also, do not touch your mouth or eyes while handling chillies – the burning will be intense. Whole chillies can be seeded to make them a little less hot. Regulate the quantity of chilli recommended in the recipes according to how much you can bear, and do not forget to tell your guests if you have left a whole chilli lurking in the curry.

You can now buy fresh chillies at many grocery shops and supermarkets. If you live a long way from a regular supplier of chillies, buy them when you see them, wash them, dry them, put them in a jar and fill it to the brim with oil. Screw the lid on tightly and keep them in a cool dark place. This is a very good way of storing them, and you get a flavoured oil out of it too. Otherwise chillies go mouldy quite quickly. If one is mouldy, all the others will be infected too and the whole lot should be thrown away.

Chillies go red as they ripen, so dried chillies are always red. They are dropped into hot oil to release their aroma before other ingredients are added.

Chilli powder is very hot indeed because it is made from the crushed seeds of the chilli, its hottest part. A blend of chilli, garlic, cumin and oregano is also sold as chilli powder.

Cinnamon (*Dalchini*)
Cinnamon has a rich, warm flavour. It is available as a powder but is much better bought in sticks. You can then break off a piece and add it to the curry. It should be discarded before serving. A lot of cinnamon is grown in Sri Lanka and it is the inner bark of a tree related to the laurel. The outer bark is scraped off and the inner bark peeled off in strips and rolled into sticks, which are then dried.

Cloves (*Luong*)
Cloves are the flower buds of an evergreen of the myrtle family. They have been used in India for thousands of years, not only in cookery, but to sweeten the breath and to relieve the pain of toothache. They contain a mild anaesthetic. Cloves are best bought whole and ground, if necessary, at home with a pestle and mortar. Whole cloves are not eaten, but left on the side of the plate.

Coconut (*Narial*)
Fresh coconut may be grated and frozen. You can buy desiccated coconut in packets in Indian shops or supermarkets, and this can be used if the fresh variety is not available. (For how to prepare coconut, see page 23.)

Coriander (*Daniya*)
The English name for this spice comes for the Greek *koros*, meaning "bug". They are small ridged seeds, light brown in colour, and can be easily squashed under the thumb. They are used powdered or whole.

Fresh green coriander (*Hari daniya*)
The leaves of the coriander plant are rather like those of flat-leaved parsley, but darker and more brilliant. Fresh coriander can be quite expensive to buy, but it is just as easily grown as parsley and can be used in the same way, on English as well as Indian dishes. The leaves have a very distinctive bitter-sweet taste. The best way of keeping this herb is in a jug of water in the fridge. Tired leaves can be revived by immersing in cold water for an hour, but do not keep them in water as they will go slimy.

Cumin (*Jeera*)
Cumin seeds are long and slim, similar to caraway seeds, but have a distinctive warm aroma. They are used either whole or ground, and can be bought ground. However, it is best to buy them whole and grind your own at home, as the ground spice loses its flavour quite quickly. Cumin is often used roasted. Drop the whole seeds into a hot dry pan and cook until the roasted fragrance emerges. Shake the pan to prevent sticking. The seeds can be stored whole, or ground in a coffee grinder and stored or used immediately.

Curry leaves (*Kari pulia or Neem*)
These are small grey-greenish leaves, a bit like bay, and are grown in many Indian gardens. They can be used fresh or dried; the dried ones can be crumbled on to food, and their aroma is released by its heat and moisture. They are sometimes fried in the oil the food is cooked in, and then discarded. They can also be eaten.

Food colourings
Turmeric and saffron will colour food yellow, but you can also buy a vegetable colouring that has no taste.

Red food colouring is used on tandoori chicken.

Fennel (*Soonf*)
Small oval seeds, greenish and with an anise flavour, they have digestive properties, and are sometimes served roasted at the end of an Indian meal. Used sparingly, they give warmth and sweetness to curries.

Fenugreek (*Methi*)
These tawny coloured seeds are chunky and very hard. Their bitter taste and aroma is released only by cooking. In powdered form, fenugreek is one of the main ingredients of curry powders. It is used sparingly on its own. The leaves of the plant, which is related to spinach, are used in India as a herb.

Garam masala
Garam masala, meaning "hot spices", is a mixture of ground spices that is used sparingly, sprinkled either on a finished dish or on to the food just before it has finished cooking. It is far better to grind your own spices than to buy the mixture ready-ground. Bought garam masala often contains inferior quality spices and will not keep its flavour for long.

For homemade garam masala, grind together the

cardamom seeds from 10 pods, 25 g/1 oz cinnamon stick, 6 cloves and 6–8 whole black peppercorns. Store in an airtight jar in a cool place.

Ghee

This is clarified butter and can be made at home (see page 21). The advantage of using ghee is that it can be heated to a very high temperature without burning, and so is useful for browning onions in order to give a sauce a good rich colour, and for sizzling spices before the main ingredients are added to the pan. Because the milk solids have been removed from ghee, it will keep well without being refrigerated. Many people prefer to use unsaturated fats and oils instead of ghee or butter.

Ginger

You can buy ginger ground (*soondth*) or fresh (*adrak*). The ground type is the same as that used in baking. The fresh "root" ginger is actually a rhizome, and is fawn in colour and knobbly. Inside, the ginger is hard, yellow and fibrous. It is easiest to cook with, once peeled and grated. You can also chop it if you are going to liquidize it with other ingredients. Fresh ginger can be kept wrapped in foil in the

freezer or in a pot of sandy soil, kept fairly dry. It has quite a hot pungent flavour and should be used sparingly.

Mango powder (*Amchur*)

Unripe mangoes are sliced and dried, then powdered and sold as amchur. Amchur has a tart taste. If you are unable to find it, use a dash of lemon or lime instead.

Mustard seeds (*Rai*)

There are both white and black mustard seeds – the black contain a higher proportion of the volatile mustard oil. When dropped into hot oil, the mustard seeds pop, releasing their flavour. It is best to put a lid over the pan while you do this, or they will fly all over the kitchen. You can use this technique when shallow-frying Western food to add extra aroma.

Nutmeg and mace
(*Jaiphal and Javitri*)

Mace is the fleshy lattice-like covering of the nutmeg, which is golden brown in colour. It is sold whole or powdered. Nutmegs are best bought whole and freshly grated at home.

Oil

Mustard oil, derived from the seeds of the mustard

plant, is very popular with south Indian cooks, especially for pickling. This, and coconut oil, can be bought at specialist Indian shops. Coconut oil is stirred together with a little warm water to release its aroma before use.

Groundnut oil, also called arachide oil, is suitable for Indian cooking, as is the oil labelled simply "vegetable oil".

Paprika

Paprika is the ground seeds from the capsicum or sweet pepper. It is milder than chilli powder or cayenne.

Peppercorns (*Mirchi*)

Peppercorns grow on large bushes in Malabar, on the west coast of India. They are picked by hand just before they are ripe, when they are still green, then left in the sun to dry and become black and crinkly. White peppercorns are the mature fruit, left to ripen on the bush, with the outer husk removed. This is traditionally done by immersing sacks of peppercorns in running streams. Bacteria get to work and loosen the husks and the water finishes the job. The peppercorns are then trodden in vats, like grapes, to rid them of the final traces of husk.

Black pepper is more

aromatic; white pepper is stronger and hotter. Black pepper should always be bought whole and freshly ground over your food as it loses its aroma fast.

Poppy seeds (*Khus-khus*)

It is the milky juice in the poppy's seed pod from which opium is derived – the seeds themselves have no narcotic properties. They are small, black and hard. There is also a white type.

Saffron (*Zaffran*)

Saffron is the most

Left Selection of Spices
*1 asafoetida, 2 garam masala,
3 turmeric, 4 ground
cinnamon, 5 black
peppercorns, 6 poppy seeds,
7 nutmeg, 8 cassia, 9 ground*

*ginger, 10 crushed red chillies,
11 fenugreek, 12 cumin,
13 black mustard seeds,
14 paprika, 15 cardamom,
16 mustard seeds, 17 saffron,
18 cloves.*

Roast together the first four ingredients and set them aside. Then roast each of the remaining ingredients separately. (Some take very little roasting before the fragrance emerges and would burn if roasted with the rest.) Now grind all the roasted spices together to a fine powder and store in a screw-topped jar.

Tamarind (*Amli*)
A tamarind looks a little like a cinnamon-coloured pod of broad beans. They grow on tall trees and are peeled and seeded when ripe. The fruit is then squashed into bricks and this is how you buy it. It has a very tart citric flavour and if you cannot find it, use a dash of lemon or lime instead. (For preparing tamarind juice, see page 22.)

Turmeric (*Haldi*)
Turmeric is a rhizome related to ginger. Bought as a powder, it gives curries their characteristic golden yellow colour. It has a delicate taste and is mildly antiseptic, although it becomes bitter if too much is used. Indians often use turmeric with beans because of its digestive properties.

Vindaloo paste
This is a very hot spicy paste. Chillies may be used with their seeds if you like particularly fiery food. In western India the Christians eat pork vindaloo. For those not permitted pork, vindaloo goes well with beef, lamb or prawns.

10 red chillies
50 g/2 oz fresh ginger, finely grated
12 cloves garlic, 4 chopped and 8 thinly sliced
½ tsp fenugreek seeds
1 tsp mustard seeds
1 tsp cumin seeds
2–3 tbsp white wine vinegar
5–6 tbsp oil
225 g/8 oz onion, chopped
450 g/1 lb tomatoes, peeled
cardamon seeds from 8 pods

Grind or pound the chillies, half of the ginger, chopped garlic, fenugreek, mustard and cumin, and mix them to a paste with the vinegar. Do not add any water. Heat the oil and fry the onion until golden, then add the tomatoes and squash them into a paste as you cook. Stir in the spicy vinegar paste you have already made, add the remaining spices and fry until the oil runs out of them. The paste is then ready. Allow it to cool and store in an airtight container in a cool dark place.

expensive spice of all. It is the filaments from a specially cultivated crocus – 75,000 stamens are needed to make 100 g/ 4 oz of the spice. It is grown in Kashmir and used on festive occasions to give food a bright yellow colour and a distinctive aroma. The filaments can be lightly roasted, crumbled in a little hot water and left to infuse to bring out their full strength. Buy saffron only from a reputable spice dealer or you may get an adulterated product, or something that is not saffron at all, especially if you buy it ready-powdered.

Sambar powder
This is a delicious aromatic spice mix used in a number of recipes in this book.

100 g/4 oz coriander seeds
1 tsp asafoetida
4 whole red chillies
6 curry leaves
25 g/1 oz polished split black lentils (urid dal)
25 g/1 oz channa dal
25 g/1 oz fenugreek seeds
1 tbsp mustard seeds
4–6 whole black peppercorns

Pulses (Dals)

There are many varieties available in India and most of them can be found in Britain at Indian grocery stores and health food shops.

Arhar dal Also called toor or toovar dal, this is the main dal used in Southern India.

Channa dal These are similar to split peas, but slightly smaller.

Chole *(Chick peas)* Beige, round, dried peas. Should be soaked overnight to reduce the cooking time. Chick pea flour is called gram, and is widely used in cooking.

Lobia *(Black-eyed peas)* White, kidney-shaped beans with a black "eye". Popular in the North.

Masoor dal *(Split red lentils)* Salmon-coloured, small, flat, round lentils which cook easily.

Mater *(Split peas)* Round, yellow lentils which are uniform in size.

Moong dal
Small, yellow, split lentils. Bean sprouts are made by sprouting these beans.

Rajma *(Red kidney beans)* Large, dark red kidney-shaped beans. Should be soaked overnight to reduce cooking time.

Toovar dal See Arhar dal.

Urid dal *(Black gram)* The bean is reddish black in colour, is very small in size and takes a long time to cook. The split urid dal is pale cream in colour. It is usually soaked and ground to a paste.

1 Pumpkin	*4 White radish*
2 Spinach	*5 Okra*
3 Doddy	*6 Bitter gourd*

Moong dal *Masoor dal*

Chole *Channa dal*

Rajma *Urid dal*

Lobia *Mater*

Indian cuisine uses a wide variety of vegetables (left) – some familiar and others more unusual. All are available fresh from Indian grocers. Pulses (above) can be bought in most supermarkets and health food shops.

Special techniques

Adding spices to hot oil (*Baghar phoron*) Oil is heated until it is very hot, and whole spices, crushed garlic or green chillies are added until the spices swell up or splutter or change colour. This is then added to a cooked dish, or vegetables, or other spices are added and cooking continues.

Dry roasting Place whole spices in a small, heavy-based frying pan and heat gently, stirring the spices constantly so that they do not burn. Soon the spices will turn a few shades darker and a lovely aroma will emerge.

Frying onions Place the oil in a frying pan or saucepan over a medium high heat. When hot add the onions, and, stirring occasionally, fry until the onions start to change colour. Lower the heat and continue to fry until they are reddish brown.

Adding yoghurt while cooking When a recipe calls for yoghurt, always whisk the yoghurt until smooth and add slowly, otherwise it curdles.

Peeling tomatoes Place the tomatoes in boiling water for 30 seconds. Drain and cool under running cold water. Peel, chop and use as required.

Cleaning chillies Pull out or slice off the stalks of the chillies and, holding them under cold running water, slit them open with a sharp knife and remove the seeds. The seeds are the hottest part of the chillies and most Indians do not remove them. Be very careful, when handling chillies, not to put your hands near your eyes as the oil will make your eyes burn.

Chillies can be stored for 12–14 days by removing the stalk of each chilli and putting them in a closed bottle in the refrigerator. When needed, wash the chillies and use as required.

SHELLING PISTACHIO NUTS

1 Pour boiling water over the nuts and leave for 30 seconds.

2 Drain and immerse in cold water.

3 The skin now peels away quite easily.

CLEANING A CHILLI

1 Slice off the stalk end of the chilli and hold it under cold running water. With a sharp knife, slit it open from top to bottom.

2 Remove all the seeds, keeping the chilli under the running water to prevent the oil splashing into your eyes.

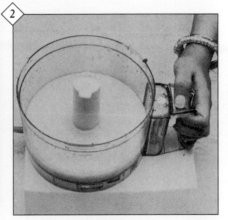

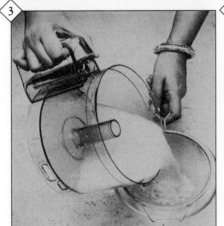

MAKING COCONUT MILK

1 Add hot water to the grated coconut.

2 Blend the mixture until it is very smooth.

3 Pour through a sieve and collect the milk.

4 Squeeze the remaining milk out by hand.

Basic recipes

Home-made Cottage Cheese
(Panir)

3.5 litres/6¼ pt milk
about 250 ml/8 fl oz warm water
about 5 tbsp white vinegar

1 Bring the milk to the boil, stirring constantly, over a high heat. Remove from heat.

2 Combine the water and vinegar.

3 Slowly add the vinegar solution to the boiled milk, stirring with a wooden spoon. As soon as the milk curdles do not add any more. (The curd and whey will separate.)

4 Place three or four layers of cheesecloth in a sieve and strain the curdled milk through them. Tie up the ends of the cheesecloth and squeeze out as much of the liquid as possible. Hang it up to drain thoroughly.

When adding the water and vinegar mixture to the milk, do not add more than necessary as this tends to harden the panir. Use in salt or sweet dishes.

MAKING PANIR

1 Bring the milk to the boil and slowly add the water and vinegar.

2 Stop adding vinegar as soon as the milk curdles.

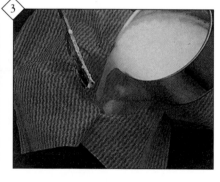

3 Strain the curdled milk through several layers of cloth.

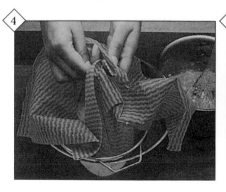

4 Tie the ends of the cloth and squeeze the liquid out.

5 Hang the cheese up to drain.

Yoghurt
(Dahi)

1.2 litres/2 pt milk
2½ tbsp yoghurt

1 Bring the milk to the boil, stirring constantly.

2 Remove the heat and let it cool so that it feels just warm.

3 Place the yoghurt in a large bowl and whisk until smooth. Slowly add the lukewarm milk and stir gently. Cover the bowl and leave in a warm place overnight. Chill and use as required.

Yoghurt is used a great deal in Indian cooking to marinate meats and to give flavour to certain types of curry.

As yoghurt is very refreshing and cool it is eaten at most meals in certain parts of the country, particularly in the north. It is eaten either plain or with some seasoning or vegetables added to it. In Bengal, sweetened yoghurt is eaten as a dessert.

On a hot day it can be mixed with water to make a refreshing drink called *lassi*.

Most families in India make their own yoghurt at home, though it is easily available in the shops.

Once you have made some yoghurt you can keep a little aside for the next batch, if you are going to make it within a day or two.

Clarified Butter
(Ghee)

450 g/1 lb unsalted butter

Ghee can be bought at any Indian grocery store, but home-made ghee has a special flavour.

1 Heat the butter in a saucepan over a low heat. Let it simmer until all the white residue turns golden and settles at the bottom.

2 Remove from the heat, strain and cool.

3 Pour into an airtight bottle and store in a cool place.

Keeps for 1–2 months.

Tamarind Juice
(*Imli ki rus*)

75 g/3 oz dried tamarind
250 ml/8 fl oz hot water

1 Soak the tamarind in the water for about 30 minutes.

2 Squeeze the pulp well to draw out all the juice. Strain and use as required.

By altering the amount of water you can change the consistency.

Mixed Spice
(*Garam masala*)

3 tbsp cardamom seeds
3 x 2.5 cm/1 in pieces of cinnamon stick
1 ½ tsp cumin seeds
½ tbsp black peppercorns
½ tsp cloves
¼ of a nutmeg

1 Grind all the spices together until they are finely ground.

2 Store in a spice bottle until required.

The ingredients may be added in different proportions to suit individual taste.

Onion Mixture

2 large onions
3 tomatoes
3.5 cm/1 ½ in ginger
5 cloves garlic
3–4 green chillies
4 tsp white vinegar

1 Blend all the ingredients together until you have a smooth paste.

2 Pour into an airtight bottle and keep in the refrigerator until needed. It will keep for up to two weeks.

Fresh garlic (below) and cardamom (left) are widely used in Indian cuisine.

Coconut Milk
(*Narial ki dudh*)

When buying a coconut, shake it to make sure it is full of water. The more liquid it has, the fresher it is. (This liquid is not coconut milk, it is coconut water, and can be served as a drink when chilled.)

To open the coconut Take a screwdriver and punch two holes in the eyes of the coconut and drain off all the liquid. Place in a pre-heated oven at 190°C/375°F/Gas 5 for 15–20 minutes. While the coconut is still hot, hit it with a hammer to split it and the flesh should come away from the shell.

To grate Peel off the brown skin from the coconut flesh and grate either with a hand grater or in a food processor.

To make coconut milk Combine the grated coconut with 500 ml/18 fl oz of very hot water and blend. Pass this liquid through a sieve and squeeze the pulp to draw out all the liquid. This is known as thick coconut milk. The pulp is normally thrown away, but a few recipes may call for thin coconut milk, in which case the process is repeated using about 500 ml/18 fl oz of hot water added to the coconut pulp. Blend the mixture and strain.

Thick milk has a lot more flavour than thin milk.

A quick method of making coconut milk is to blend together 75 g/3 oz of creamed coconut with 500 ml/18 fl oz of hot water. Creamed coconut is available in supermarkets in 200 g/7 oz slabs. It keeps in the refrigerator for 2–3 months.

Roasted Cumin
(*Sukha bhuna jeera*)

2 tbsp whole cumin seeds

1 Place the cumin seeds in a small pan over a medium heat and dry roast them, stirring constantly. The seeds will then turn a few shades darker. (Take care not to burn them.)

2 Cool and grind finely. Store in a spice bottle until required.

Coriander seeds and dried red chillies can be roasted and ground in a similar manner and stored.

The Indian kitchen

Indian food can be cooked easily in a modern kitchen and you do not need to go out to get a lot of equipment. However, you may be interested to know about some of the more traditional implements and utensils of the Indian kitchen.

A chula This is a hollow cube with a hole towards the bottom through which fuel is fed, and a hole at the top which acts as the burner. Midway there are four or five iron rods which act as a bracket to hold the coal. The chula must have mud placed regularly on the inside and outside, so that it does not lose its shape. The mud is then left to dry out. There is a special technique to placing the mud, to ensure that after it dries out there are no cracks. In the cities, gas or electric stoves are often used.

A degchi This is a pan without handles, made of polished brass, stainless steel or other metals. The lid of the degchi is slightly dipped so that sometimes live coal can be placed on it to cook food slowly or keep food warm. Ordinary saucepans with lids can be used in the same way and the oven can be used to cook food slowly or to keep it warm.

A karai This is found in every Indian kitchen. It is a deep, concave metallic dish with two handles – one on each side. It looks like a Chinese wok but it is a little more rounded. It is used for deep frying. A deep fryer or saucepan or frying pan can be used if you do not have a karai.

A tava This is made from cast iron, is slightly concave, and is about 25 cm/10 in in diameter. It is ideal for making chappatis or parathas because it distributes the heat evenly. A heavy-based frying pan will serve the same purpose.

Tongs These are used to remove a karai from the fire, or to remove the hot lid from the degchi. To remove the degchi from the fire it is normally held at either side with a cloth.

Metallic stirrers These are used in India because the pans are not non-stick. Use wooden spoons when using non-stick pans. Wooden spoons are easier to use as they do not get hot, although if left in hot oil they tend to burn.

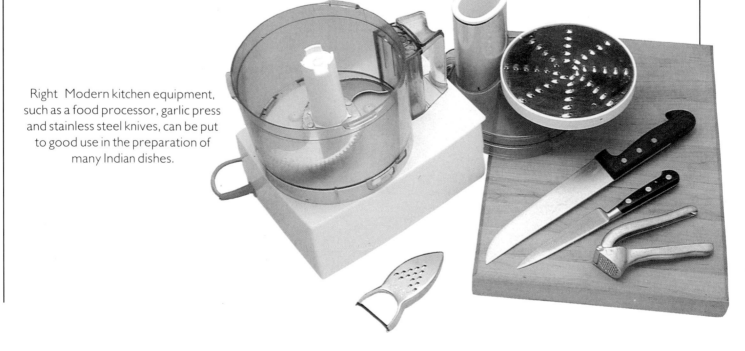

Right Modern kitchen equipment, such as a food processor, garlic press and stainless steel knives, can be put to good use in the preparation of many Indian dishes.

A thick stone slab This is used with a round stone roller like a rolling pin for grinding. Whole spices are ground with a little water; if dry ground spice is required a mortar and pestle is used. Lentils are also ground on the slab.

A tandoor This is a clay oven used in northern India. Tandoori chicken, whole or in pieces, different kinds of breads and kebabs are baked in this oven. It is about 91 cm–1.2 m/3–4 ft deep and about 60 cm/2 ft wide on top with a hole of 30 cm/12 in diameter through which the food is put for cooking. It is fuelled by wood and coal and intensive heat builds up inside. This oven has mud patted on the inside and outside and it must be allowed to dry out. The chicken or the kebabs are marinated and then skewered and placed in the

Above The tandoor or clay oven is used widely in the northern regions. Tandoori meats are marinated and then dry-cooked at speed in the intense heat of the tandoor.

tandoor; the intensity of the heat cooks a whole chicken in a matter of minutes.

When bread is baked in a tandoor, the dough is slapped on to the inside of the oven and when bubbles form, which is in a matter of a few seconds, the bread is cooked. It does not need to be turned over.

Tandoori chicken can be cooked easily in the modern oven, and then put under a very hot grill for a few minutes to dry out. It can also taste excellent barbecued.

An electric coffee grinder In the modern kitchen, this can be used to grind spices. A blender or food processor may be used to blend onions, lentils and rice. The food processor can be used to make the dough for most of the breads and to save time when grating vegetables.

Left Traditional kitchen equipment includes the karai, shown on the left of the picture with tongs to lift it from the heat and a wooden stirrer. The heavy frying pan and saucepan on the right of the picture are suitable modern substitutes for the tava and the degchi.

Presentation is an important part of good Indian cooking, and imaginative use of garnishes can make an ordinary dish into something really special. Tomatoes, lettuce and coriander leaves are often used to add colour and a crisp texture.

Top left Red Peppers Stuffed with Vegetables, Centre left Sardines in a Thick Spicy Sauce, Below left Baked Fish Stuffed with Mushrooms, Top right Vegetable Curry, Kerala Style, Centre right Yellow Rice with Hard-Boiled Eggs, Below right Pumpkin Halva.

Moong Dal
Split yellow bean, cleaned of husk.

Chole (Chickpeas)
Rounded, beige unsplit peas.

Musoor Dal (Split Red Lentils)
Pink in colour, cook easily.

Channa Dal
Smaller in size than split peas,
yellow in colour.

Rajma (Red Kidney Beans)
Cook more easily if soaked
overnight first.

Lobia (Black Eyed Beans)
Small beige beans with a black dot.
Have a smoky flavour.

Urid Dal (Dehulled Split Matpe)
Small whitish lentil.

Matar Dal (Split Peas)
Round yellow lentils, uniform in size.

Pulses

. . . .

India has over 60 varieties of pulses which provide a primary source of protein for her millions of vegetarians. When cooked, they can be left whole or puréed, making them extremely versatile as ingredients for curries, stuffings and patties. They can even be roasted or deep-fried for garnishes or snacks.

To cook pulses, first pick them over and remove any foreign bodies. The larger varieties should be soaked overnight (at least 10 hours). If you are in a hurry, you can bring them to the boil, continue boiling for a couple of minutes and then take the pan off the heat and leave it to stand for an hour before cooking.

Lentils Flavoured with Garlic
(Rasam)

SERVES 2
100 g/4 oz toovar dal
900 ml/1 ½ pt water
pinch of ground turmeric
1 tsp salt
2 tsp cumin seeds
1 tsp coriander seeds
½ tsp peppercorns
3–4 diced red chillies
250 ml/8 fl oz tamarind juice
   (see page 22)
15 curry leaves
5 cloves garlic, crushed
1 tomato, chopped
1 tsp ghee (see page 21)
¼ tsp cumin seeds

1 Wash the toovar dal in several changes of water and bring to a boil in a large saucepan with the measured amount of water, turmeric and salt. Cover, leaving the lid slightly open, and simmer for about 30 minutes until the dal is soft. Blend until smooth.

2 In the meantime, dry roast the cumin, coriander, peppercorns and red chillies and grind finely.

3 Mix the tamarind juice, the powdered spices, 10 curry leaves and garlic and bring to a boil. Simmer until it has reduced to half the amount.

4 Add the cooked dal and tomato and simmer for 5 minutes.

5 In a small saucepan, heat the ghee until very hot, add the ¼ tsp of cumin seeds and the remaining curry leaves and let them sizzle for 5–6 seconds. Add to the cooked dal. Serve very hot with rice or as a soup.

Lentils with Vegetables I
(Kootu)

SERVES 4
225 g/8 oz toovar dal, washed
900 ml/1 ½ pt water
½ tsp turmeric
1 tsp salt
75 g/3 oz carrots, scraped and diced
50 g/2 oz peas (fresh or frozen)
100 g/4 oz French beans, cut into
   2.5 cm/1 in lengths
1 tbsp oil
1 tbsp urid dal
1 tsp peppercorns
2 dried red chillies, broken in half
10–12 curry leaves
4 tbsp grated coconut
175 ml/6 fl oz milk

1 Place the toovar dal, water, turmeric and salt in a saucepan and bring to a boil. Cover and simmer for about 35–40 minutes until the dal is soft. Add the vegetables and continue to cook until they are tender.

2 While the toovar dal is being cooked, heat the oil in a small saucepan and fry the urid dal, peppercorns, red chillies, curry leaves and coconut until the dal and coconut turn golden. Grind to a paste.

3 When the dal and vegetables are cooked, add the paste and milk and continue to cook for 5–10 minutes. Serve hot with rice.

Below Lentils with vegetables I/Kootu

Special Curried Chick Peas
(*Channa curry*)

SERVES 4

225 g/8 oz chick peas
1.2 litres/2 pt water
½ tsp bicarbonate of soda
100 g/4 oz butter or ghee
1 onion
2 or 3 bay leaves
cardamom seeds from 1 pod
2.5 cm/1 in cinnamon stick
3 cloves
15 g/½ oz fresh ginger, finely grated
1 tsp fennel seeds
3 cloves garlic, chopped
175 g/6 oz tomatoes, peeled and
    chopped
1 tsp chilli powder
1½ tsp ground cumin
leaves from 1–2 sprigs coriander
½ tsp paprika
2 tsp ground coriander
1 tbsp lemon juice
salt

1 Pick over the chick peas and wash thoroughly. Soak in water for at least 10 hours. Drain and cook in the measured water with the bicarbonate of soda for 1–1½ hours, depending on the age of the peas, until tender but not soft.

2 Heat three-quarters of the butter or ghee in a good-sized pan and add the onion, bay leaves, cardamom seeds, cinnamon, cloves, ginger, fennel seeds, garlic and tomatoes. Fry until the onion is golden, squashing the tomato under the back of a wooden spoon to make a thick paste.

3 Add the chilli powder, half the cumin, the coriander leaves and paprika and cook for 3–4 minutes, stirring occasionally.

4 Add the cooked chick peas with about 120 ml/¼ pt of their cooking liquor and cook over a low heat for 8–10 minutes.

5 In a separate pan, heat the remaining butter or ghee and when hot, add the remaining ground cumin. Fry for a few seconds, until the fragrance emerges, and add to the chick peas.

6 Sprinkle on the ground coriander and lemon juice, and add salt to taste.

Steamed Rice and Lentil Cake
(*Idli*)

SERVES 4
90 g/2½ oz urid dal, washed
200 g/7 oz rice, washed
good pinch of baking powder
pinch of salt

1 Soak the dal and rice separately in plenty of water for 4–5 hours. Drain.

2 In a liquidizer or food processor, grind the dal to a fine paste, adding a little water if necessary.

3 Grind the rice coarsely, adding a little water if necessary.

4 Mix the dal and rice together thoroughly, cover and then leave in a warm place overnight to let them ferment.

5 Mix in the baking powder and salt.

6 Fill the idli vessel* with the fermented mixture and steam for about 10 minutes until an inserted skewer comes out clean. Serve with Lentils with Vegetables II (see page 32).

* If you do not have a idli vessel, you can use egg poachers or custard cups.

Below Steamed rice and lentil cakes/ Idli, served with Lentils with vegetables II and Coconut chutney

Lentils with Vegetables II
(*Sambar*)

SERVES 4
225 g/8 oz toovar dal, washed
1 litre/1¾ pt water
2 tsp salt
½ tsp ground turmeric
1½ tbsp oil
4 tsp coriander seeds
1 tsp channa dal
1 tsp urid dal
6 dried red chillies
pinch of fenugreek seeds
good pinch of asafoetida
350 g/12 oz aubergine, cut into
    1 cm/½ in pieces
90 g/2½ oz French beans, cut into
    4 cm/1½ in lengths
6–8 shallots, peeled
120 ml/4 fl oz tamarind juice
    (see page 22)
1 tsp mustard seeds
8–10 curry leaves

1 Place the toovar dal, water, 1 tsp of salt and turmeric in a large saucepan and bring to a boil. Lower the heat, cover, leaving the lid slightly ajar, and simmer for 35–40 minutes until the dal is soft.

2 In the meantime, heat ½ tbsp of oil in a small saucepan and fry the coriander seeds, channa dal and urid dal, 4 dried red chillies, fenugreek and asafoetida, stirring constantly, until golden. (Take care that they do not get burnt). Grind to a fine powder.

3 When the dal is soft, add the vegetables, tamarind juice and the remaining salt and continue to simmer until the vegetables are nearly tender.

4 Add the ground spices, stir well and cook for 5 minutes. Remove from the heat and put aside.

5 Heat the remaining 1 tbsp of oil in a small saucepan until very hot, add the mustard seeds and, when they stop spluttering, add the remaining dried red chillies, broken in half, and the curry leaves and let them fry for 4–5 seconds. Add this to the hot dal, give it a good stir and serve.

Stuffed, Spiced Pastries
(*Kachori*)

SERVES 4
Filling
100 g/4 oz urid dal, washed
1 tsp ghee (see page 21)
1 tsp salt
¼ tsp fennel seeds
1 cm/½ in cinnamon stick
½ black cardamom pod, skinned
6 peppercorns
pinch of asafoetida
pinch of ground ginger
¼ tsp ground cumin
½ tsp chilli powder
Dough
225 g/8 oz wholewheat flour
1 tsp salt
2 tsp melted ghee (see page 21)
120 ml/4 fl oz hot water
oil for deep frying

1 To make the filling, soak the dal in plenty of cold water overnight.

2 Drain and blend to a smooth paste, adding a little water if necessary.

3 Heat the ghee in a karai, add the dal paste and salt and, stirring constantly, fry until the mixture leaves the side and forms a lump. Keep on one side.

4 Grind together the fennel, cinnamon, black cardamom and peppercorns to a fine powder.

5 Add this and all the remaining spices to the dal and mix.

6 To make the dough, mix the wholewheat flour and salt.

7 Rub the ghee into the flour/salt mixture.

8 Add enough hot water to make a soft, pliable dough. Knead for about 10 minutes.

9 Divide the dough into 12–14 balls.

10 Take one ball, flatten slightly and make a depression in the middle with your thumb, to form a cup shape. Fill the centre with the spiced dal mixture and re-form the pastry ball, making sure that the edges are well gathered. Flatten the ball slightly between the palms of your hands.

11 Heat the oil in a karai over a medium heat and fry the kachoris a few at a time for 7–8 minutes until they are lightly browned. Serve with pickle.

Fried Lentil Cake Curry
(*Dhokkar dalna*)

SERVES 4
150 g/5 oz channa dal, washed
900 ml/1½ pt water
¾ tsp salt
½ tsp ground turmeric
1 cm/½ in ginger, grated
2 tbsp desiccated coconut
2 green chillies
150 ml/¼ pt water
200 ml/⅓ pt oil
3 medium potatoes, cut into
   2.5 cm/1 in pieces
½ tsp whole cumin seeds
2 bay leaves
1 tsp ground turmeric
½ tsp chilli powder
1½ tsp ground cumin
1 tsp ground coriander
½ tsp salt
2 tomatoes, chopped
350 ml/12 fl oz water
1 tsp ghee
½ tsp garam masala
(see page 13)

1 Soak the dal in 900 ml/1½ pt water overnight. Drain.

2 Mix the drained dal with ¾ tsp salt, ½ tsp turmeric, ginger, coconut, green chillies and 150 ml/¼ pt water in a blender until you have a smooth creamy mixture.

3 In a karai, heat 120 ml/4 fl oz of the oil over medium heat and fry the dal mixture until it leaves the side and a ball forms. Spread 1 cm/½ in thick on a greased plate. Cool. Cut into 2.5 cm/1 in squares.

4 Heat the rest of the oil in a karai over medium high heat and fry the dal squares a few at a time until golden brown. Set aside.

5 Fry the potatoes until lightly browned. Set aside.

6 Lower the heat to medium, add the whole cumin seeds and bay leaves and let them sizzle for a few seconds.

7 Add the turmeric, chilli, coriander, salt and tomatoes and fry for 2 minutes. Add the water and bring to boil.

8 Add the potatoes, cover and cook for 10 minutes. Add the fried dal squares, cover again and cook until the potatoes are tender.

9 Add the ghee and sprinkle on garam masala. Remove from the heat. Serve hot with rice or pillau.

Below Fried lentil cake curry/
Dhokkar dalna

Curried Chick Peas with Coconut
(Channa curry)

SERVES 4
225 g/8 oz chick peas
4–5 tbsp butter or ghee
1 tsp mustard seeds
1 onion, finely chopped
1 tbsp finely grated fresh ginger
1 green chilli, chopped
4–6 curry leaves
75 g/3 oz grated fresh coconut
salt

1 Pick over the chick peas, wash thoroughly and soak in water for at least 10 hours. Cook in fresh water for 1–1½ hours, depending on the age of the chick peas, until tender but not soft.

2 Heat the butter or ghee in a pan and add the mustard seeds. Let them sizzle for a few seconds until they have all popped.

3 Add the onion and fry until golden.

4 Drain the chick peas, reserving the cooking liquor. Add the chick peas to the pan with the ginger, green chilli and about 2 tbsp cooking liquor. Cover and cook over low heat, stirring occasionally, for 10 minutes, until the chick peas have absorbed the flavours of the sauce.

5 Stir in the curry leaves and grated coconut and add salt to taste.

Lentils cooked with Fish Heads
(Mooror dal)

SERVES 4
225 g/8 oz green lentils
about 1.5 litre/2½ pt water
¼ tsp ground turmeric
1 tsp salt
4 tbsp oil
2 fish heads, quartered
3 green chillies
2 dried red chillies
1 medium onion, chopped
¼ tsp chilli powder
4 cardamom pods
5 cm/2 in cinnamon stick
2 bay leaves
good pinch of sugar

1 Dry roast the lentils, stirring constantly, until golden brown.

2 Wash the lentils in several changes of water. Bring the lentils to a boil in the measured amount of water with the turmeric and salt.

3 Throw away the scum, lower the heat, cover, leaving the lid slightly open, and simmer for about 1 hour. Put aside.

4 Heat the oil in a pan and fry the fish heads until golden brown.

5 Drain the fish heads and add to the lentils. Put the remaining oil aside. Bring the lentils to the boil again, add the green chillies, lower the heat and simmer for about 15 minutes.

6 In a small pan, heat the remaining oil again until very hot. Add the dried red chillies and fry for 4–5 seconds. Add the onion and stir fry until golden brown.

7 Add the chilli powder, cardamom, cinnamon, bay leaves and sugar and fry for a few seconds.

8 Add to the lentils and stir thoroughly.

Dal Curry I

SERVES 2
175 g/6 oz toovar dal
900 ml/1 ½ pt water
2 tbsp oil
½ tsp mustard seeds
½ tsp cumin seeds
1 small onion, finely chopped
leaves from 1–2 sprigs coriander
2 tomatoes, peeled and chopped
½ tsp turmeric
1 clove garlic, finely chopped
2 green chillies, sliced
salt

1 Pick over the dal and wash it well. Bring the water to the boil, add the dal and simmer for about 15 minutes, until you can crush the dal with the back of a wooden spoon. Set aside, covered.

2 Heat the oil in a frying pan and add the mustard seeds. Sizzle for a few seconds until all the seeds have popped.

3 Add the cumin seeds, onion and half the coriander leaves and fry, stirring, until the onion is golden.

4 Add the tomato, turmeric, garlic and chilli, stirring well and mashing the tomato with the spices to make a paste.

5 Add the dal with a little of its cooking water. Stir well, heat through and add salt to taste. Garnish with the remaining coriander leaves.

Dal Curry II

SERVES 4
350 g/12 oz toovar dal
1.2 litres/2 pt boiling water
50 g/2 oz butter or ghee
½ tsp cumin seeds
1 ½ tbsp gram flour
salt
leaves from 1 sprig of coriander, finely chopped
1–2 green chillies, chopped

1 Pick over the dal and wash it well. Add to the water and simmer for 10–15 minutes until soft. Strain off excess water and mash well or blend in a liquidizer. Set aside.

2 Heat the butter or ghee in a pan and when hot, fry the cumin seeds for a few seconds until their flavour emerges. Add to the dal.

3 In a small bowl, mix the gram flour with 2–3 tbsp water until it forms a smooth paste.

4 Stir the paste into the dal and simmer on a low heat, stirring occasionally, for about 5 minutes, until it is thick and soupy.

5 Stir in salt to taste and garnish with coriander leaves and green chilli.

Below Dal Curry II

Dal and Mushroom Curry
(Kumban dal)

SERVES 4

225 g/8 oz red lentils (masoor dal)

1.2 litres/2 pt water

1½ tsp turmeric

175–225 g/6–8 oz button
  mushrooms, halved

15 g/½ oz fresh ginger, finely grated

1 green chilli, sliced

225 g/8 oz onion, chopped

1 tbsp sambar powder (see page 15)

2 tbsp grated or desiccated coconut

225 g/8 oz tomatoes, peeled and
  chopped

2 tbsp oil

1 tsp mustard seeds

4–6 curry leaves

salt

1 Pick over the dal and wash it thoroughly. Cook in the water with the turmeric for 10–15 minutes, until it can be crushed under the back of a wooden spoon.

2 Add the mushrooms, ginger, chilli and half of the onion, and cook for a further 10 minutes.

3 Meanwhile, blend the sambar powder with the coconut in a liquidizer, add to the curry with the tomato and cook for a further 6–8 minutes, until the sauce is thick and smooth.

4 Heat the oil in a pan, add the mustard seeds and let them sizzle for a few seconds until they have all popped.

5 Add the curry leaves and remaining onion and fry until the onion is golden. Add to the curry with salt to taste.

Below Dal and mushroom curry/
Kumban dal

Red Lentils with Fried Onions
(*Masoor dal*)

SERVES 2

200 g/7 oz red lentils, washed
1 litre/1¾ pt water
¼ tsp ground turmeric
1½ tsp ground cumin
2 tomatoes, chopped
½ tsp salt
2–3 green chillies
1 tbsp coriander leaves, chopped
3 tbsp ghee (see page 21)
3 cloves garlic, crushed
1 onion, finely sliced

1 Bring the lentils to the boil in the measured amount of water in a large saucepan. Remove any scum that forms.

2 Add the turmeric, cumin and tomatoes, and mix with the lentils.

3 Lower the heat, partially cover and simmer the lentils for about 40 minutes until tender. Add the salt, chillies and coriander leaves and mix in with the lentils. Remove from the heat.

4 In a small pan, heat the ghee. Add the garlic and onion and fry until golden brown.

5 Pour over the lentils and serve with rice.

Below Red lentils with fried onions/ Masoor dal

Dal and Coconut Curry
(Dal narial)

SERVES 2

175 g/6 oz toovar dal
900 ml/1½ pt water
1½ tsp turmeric
1½ tsp chilli powder
1 small onion, finely chopped
2–3 tbsp grated coconut
1 tomato, peeled and chopped
2 tbsp oil
1 tsp mustard seeds
4–6 curry leaves
salt

1 Pick over the dal and wash it well. Bring the water to the boil, add the dal and simmer for 10–15 minutes, until soft and mushy.

2 Stir in the turmeric and chilli powder, cover and keep hot over a low heat.

3 Put half the onion with the coconut in a liquidizer, add 1 tbsp water and blend until smooth. Stir into the dal with the tomato.

4 Heat the oil in a pan and add the mustard seeds. When all the seeds have popped, add the remaining onion and fry until golden. Add to the dal.

5 Stir in the curry leaves and salt to taste.

Green Lentil Curry I
(*Moong dal*)

SERVES 2

200 g/7 oz whole green lentils
   (moong dal)

1.4 litres/2½ pt water

¼ tsp ground turmeric

1 tsp ground cumin

2 tomatoes, chopped

1 tsp salt

1 tbsp ghee (see page 21)

¾ tsp whole cumin seeds

2 dried red chillies

2 bay leaves

2.5 cm/1 inch cinnamon stick

4 cardamoms

1 Heat a saucepan and dry roast the lentils, stirring constantly until all the lentils turn light brown.

2 Wash the lentils in several changes of water and bring to boil in the measured amount of water in a large saucepan. Skim off any scum that forms.

3 Lower the heat, add the turmeric, cumin, tomatoes and salt and partially cover and simmer for about 1 hour 15 minutes until the lentils are soft.

4 In a small pan, heat the ghee over medium heat, add the cumin seeds, red chillies, bay leaves, cinnamon stick and cardamoms and let them sizzle for a few seconds.

5 Add the hot ghee and spices to the lentils and stir. Serve with rice.

Below Green lentil curry I/
Moong dal

Lentils with Spicy Dumplings
(Dal dhokri)

SERVES 4
2 green chillies
1 cm/½ in ginger
225 g/8 oz toovar dal, washed
900 ml/1 ½ pt water
½ tsp ground turmeric
1 tsp salt
½ tsp sugar
2–3 tbsp lime juice

Dough
225 g/8 oz wholewheat flour
1 tbsp gram flour
½ tsp chilli powder
pinch of turmeric
pinch of asafoetida
½ tsp salt
1 tbsp oil
about 4 tbsp hot water
1 tbsp ghee (see page 21)
½ tsp mustard seeds
½ tsp whole cumin seeds
pinch of asafoetida
good pinch of cinnamon
2 tbsp grated coconut
2 tbsp chopped coriander leaves
2 tbsp ghee

1 Grind the chillies and ginger together into a paste.

2 Place the toovar dal, water, turmeric, salt and chilli and ginger paste in a large saucepan and bring to the boil. Cover, leaving the lid slightly open, and simmer for 40–45 minutes until the dal is tender. Add the sugar and lime juice and mix thoroughly. Remove from the heat and put aside.

3 To make the dough, sieve together the wholewheat flour, gram flour, chilli powder, turmeric, asafoetida and salt.

4 Rub in the oil.

5 Add enough water to make a stiff dough. Knead for 8–10 minutes until soft and smooth.

6 Divide into 4 portions. Take one, flatten slightly and roll into a round 20 cm/8 in across. Cut into small diamond shapes; do the same with the other portions.

7 In a small saucepan, heat the oil, add the mustard and cumin seeds and, as soon as the seeds start to splutter, add the asafoetida and cinnamon and fry for 2–3 seconds. Add to the dal.

8 Add the small diamond pieces of dough to the dal, bring to a boil again and boil for 12–15 minutes, stirring occasionally. (Add a little water if the dal gets too thick.)

9 Garnish with the coconut, coriander and ghee. Serve hot – this is a meal by itself.

Spicy Lentils
(Aamti)

100 g/4 oz toovar dal, washed
900 ml/1 ½ pt water
pinch of turmeric
1 tsp salt
1 tbsp oil
½ tsp mustard seeds
1 clove garlic, crushed
½ tsp whole cumin seeds
120 ml/4 fl oz tamarind juice
2 tbsp coriander leaves, chopped

1 Place the toovar dal, water, turmeric and salt in a large saucepan and bring to a boil.

2 Cover, leaving the lid slightly open and simmer the dal for about 40–45 minutes until tender. In a food processor or liquidizer, blend the dal until smooth; return to the saucepan.

3 Heat the oil in a small saucepan. Add the mustard seeds, garlic and cumin seeds and fry until the mustard seeds start to splutter.

4 Add the tamarind juice and bring to a boil, stirring constantly. Add this to the dal and mix thoroughly. Boil for 5 minutes.

5 Garnish with the coriander leaves and serve hot.

Green Lentil Curry II
(*Moong cury*)

SERVES 2
175 g/6 oz whole green lentils
   (moong dal)
100 g/4 oz butter or ghee
1 onion, finely chopped
1 green chilli, chopped
2 cloves garlic, chopped
15 g/½ oz fresh ginger, finely grated
100 g/4 oz tomatoes, peeled and
   chopped
½ tsp turmeric
½ tsp chilli powder
leaves from 1 sprig of coriander
1 tsp cumin seeds
salt

1 Pick over the lentils, wash thoroughly and soak in water for about 4 hours. Drain and cook in fresh water to cover for about 30 minutes, until tender.

2 Meanwhile, heat three-quarters of the butter or ghee in a pan, add the onion, green chilli, garlic and ginger and fry until the onion is golden.

3 Add the tomato and cook, mashing it under the back of a wooden spoon to make a paste.

4 Add the turmeric, chilli powder and coriander leaves and continue to cook until the fat runs clear of the spices.

5 Add the lentils and about 2 tbsp of their cooking liquor and cook for a further 5 minutes.

6 Meanwhile, fry the cumin seeds in the remaining butter or ghee for a few seconds, until the fragrance emerges, then add to the lentils. Add salt to taste.

Dry Sprouted Green Lentil Toran
(*Moong dal toran*)

SERVES 4
2 tbsp oil
¼ tsp asafoetida
1 tsp chilli powder
½ tsp turmeric
1 tsp ground coriander
½ tsp ground cumin
450 g/1 lb sprouted green lentils
salt
leaves from 1 sprig of coriander
1 tsp lemon juice

1 Heat the oil in a pan, add the asafoetida, chilli powder, turmeric, ground coriander and cumin, and fry for a few minutes until the fragrance emerges.

2 Add the sprouted lentils together with 2 tbsp water, ½ tsp salt and half the coriander leaves. Cook, covered, on a low heat, stirring occasionally, for about 10 minutes or until the sprouted lentils are cooked and almost all the water has evaporated.

3 Sprinkle on the lemon juice and the remaining coriander leaves. Add extra salt to taste.

Green Lentil and Banana Curry
(*Kela moong curry*)

SERVES 2
175 g/6 oz whole green lentils
   (moong dal)
900 ml/1½ pt water
1 or 2 plantains, scraped and sliced
½ tsp turmeric
1 green chill, chopped
salt
100 g/4 oz grated or desiccated
   coconut
½ tsp ground cumin
2 tbsp oil
1 tsp mustard seeds
4–6 curry leaves

1 Pick over the lentils, wash thoroughly and cook in the water for about 30 minutes until nearly done.

2 Add the plaintain, turmeric, chilli and ½ tsp salt, and continue to cook over a low heat.

3 In a liquidizer, blend the coconut with the cumin and 1–2 tbsp water to make a thick paste. Add to the lentils. Stir and cook for 3 minutes to heat through. Add a little water, if necessary, to make a thick sauce.

4 Heat the oil in a frying pan and when hot, add the mustard seeds and the curry leaves. Let them sizzle for a few seconds until all the seeds have popped, then add to the curry. Add extra salt to taste.

Channna Dal

SERVES 2
200 g/7 oz channa dal, washed
1.4 litres/2½ pt water
1½ tbsp ghee (see page 21)
¾ tsp whole cumin seeds
2 bay leaves
2 dried red chillies
5 cm/2 in cinnamon stick
4 cardamoms
¾ tsp ground turmeric
½ tsp chilli powder
1¼ tsp ground cumin
1 tsp salt
½ tsp sugar
2 tbsp desiccated coconut
1 tbsp raisins

1 Bring the dal and water to the boil in a large saucepan over medium high heat. Skim off any scum that forms.

2 Lower the heat, partially cover the pan and simmer for about 1 hour 15 minutes until soft.

3 Heat the ghee in a small pan over medium heat, add the whole cumin seeds, bay leaves, red chillies, cinnamon stick and cardamoms and allow them to sizzle for a few seconds.

4 Add the turmeric, chilli powder, ground cumin, salt and sugar and stir fry for 1 minute. Add the desiccated coconut and raisins and fry for another 1–2 minutes.

5 Mix the ghee and spices with the dal and stir. Serve with rice or Deep fried white bread (see page 148) and Spicy potatoes (see page 80).

Above Channa dal

Soured Lentils
(*Khatta moong*)

SERVES 2
100 g/4 oz whole green lentils
   (moong dal)
600 ml/1 pt water
½ tsp ground turmeric
1 tsp salt
120 ml/4 fl oz yoghurt
750 ml/1¼ pt water
2 tbsp gram flour
4 green chillies
1 cm/½ in ginger
2 tsp ghee (see page 21)
2.5 cm/1 in cinnamon stick
½ tsp cumin seeds
pinch of asafoetida
½ tsp sugar
2 tbsp coriander leaves, chopped

1 Wash the dal thoroughly. Place the dal, 600 ml/1 pt of water, pinch of turmeric and ½ tsp salt in a saucepan and bring to the boil. Lower the heat, cover, leaving the lid slightly open, and simmer until the dal has split open, but is still whole. (It should not become mushy). Drain and put aside.

2 Whisk together the yoghurt, water and gram flour until smooth.

3 Grind 2 green chillies and the ginger to a paste.

4 Heat the ghee in a large saucepan. Add 2 green chillies, broken in half, cinnamon, cumin and asafoetida and let them sizzle for 5–6 seconds.

5 Add the yoghurt mixture, the remaining turmeric and salt, sugar and the chilli and ginger paste. Stirring constantly, cook for 5–7 minutes.

6 Add the drained dal and cook for a further 5 minutes until thick. Garnish with the coriander leaves.

The yoghurt should be left at room temperature for 24 hours so that it has a slightly sour taste.

Split Peas with Vegetables
(Dal tarkari)

SERVES 4

200 g/7 oz split peas, washed

750 ml/1¼ pt water

2 tbsp ghee (see page 21)

½ tsp whole cumin seeds

2 bay leaves

2–3 green chillies, cut lengthways

275 g/10 oz potatoes, cut into
   2.5 cm/1 in pieces

75 g/3 oz peas

350 g/12 oz cauliflower, cut into
   large florets

½ tsp ground turmeric

1 tsp salt

1 In a large saucepan, bring the split peas and water to the boil. Cover and simmer for 30 minutes. Remove from the heat.

2 Heat the ghee in a large saucepan over medium high heat. Add the cumin seeds, bay leaves and green chillies and let them sizzle for a few seconds.

3 Add the potatoes, peas and cauliflower and fry for 1–2 minutes.

4 Add the boiled split peas with the water, turmeric and salt. Mix thoroughly, lower the heat and cook until the vegetables are tender. (If the dal gets too thick add a little more water.)

Below Split peas with vegetables/ Dal tarkari

Split Pea and Yam Curry
(*Koot*)

SERVES 4

225 g/8 oz yellow split peas (channa dal)

½ tsp turmeric

½ tsp chilli powder

1.2 litres/2 pt water

450 g/1 lb yams, peeled and cubed

225 g/8 oz white pumpkin or green plantain, peeled and cubed

275–350 g/10–12 oz grated fresh or dried unsweetened coconut

1 tsp cumin seeds

1 tsp mustard seeds

2–3 tbsp oil

1 red chilli pepper, cut into pieces

6–8 curry leaves

salt

1 Soak the split peas in water with the turmeric and chilli powder for about 2 hours. Drain and cook in the measured amount of water for 15–20 minutes, until the peas can be crushed with the back of a wooden spoon and most of the water has evaporated.

Below Split pea and yam curry/Koot

2 Cook the yam and pumpkin or plantain in water to cover for about 15 minutes, until tender but not soft.

3 Add the cooked peas to the vegetables over low heat, stirring occasionally.

4 Blend three-quarters of the coconut with the cumin seeds in a blender or food processor for a few seconds only, and add to the curry.

5 Fry the mustard seeds in the oil until they have all popped. Add the red chilli, curry leaves and remaining coconut. Fry for a further 3–4 minutes, stirring, then add to the curry.

6 Take the curry off the heat, cover and let stand for 3–4 minutes, then add salt to taste.

Curried Pumpkin and Black-eyed Peas
(Pethi lobia)

SERVES 4

225 g/8 oz dried black-eyed peas,
   soaked overnight
225 g/8 oz unripe red pumpkin or
   butternut squash, peeled and
   thinly sliced
2 green chilli peppers, cut into 4
   pieces
2 tbsp coconut oil
4 curry leaves
salt

1 Drain the peas and cook in fresh water for about 10 minutes, until barely tender.

2 Add the pumpkin and green chilli and cook for a further 5–7 minutes, until tender.

3 Mix the coconut oil with 1 tbsp water to release its aroma, then add to the curry with the curry leaves and salt to taste.

Right Curried pumpkin and black-
    eyed peas/Pethi lobia

Black-eyed Peas with Onions
(*Lobia aur pyaz*)

SERVES 2
200 g/7 oz black-eyed peas, washed
1.2 litres/2 pt water
2 tbsp oil
1 large onion, finely chopped
2 cloves garlic, crushed
5 mm/¼ in ginger, grated
1–2 green chillies, finely chopped
½ tsp salt
1 tsp molasses

1 Soak the beans in the water overnight.

2 Boil the beans in the water and then cover and simmer for 1 hour until tender. Drain.

3 Heat the oil in a large saucepan and fry the onion, garlic, ginger and chilli until the onions are soft.

4 Add the beans, salt and molasses and cook until all the moisture is absorbed, about 15 minutes. Serve with Chappatis (see page 146).

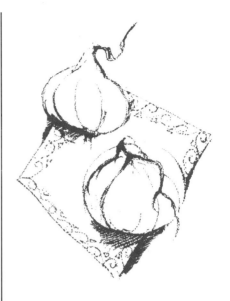

Below Black-eyed peas with onions/
Lobia aur pyaz

Above Chick peas with mango and
coconut/Aam aur narial ke channa

Chick Peas with Mango and Coconut
(*Aam aur narial ke channa*)

SERVES 2
100 g/4 oz chick peas
flesh of ½ coconut
225 g/8 oz green mango, peeled
25 g/7 oz butter or ghee
½ tsp ground cumin
salt

1 Pick over the chick peas, wash thoroughly and soak in water for at least 10 hours. Drain. Cook in fresh water for 1–1½ hours, depending on the age of the peas, until tender but not soft.

2 Chop the coconut flesh and mango into small even pieces and mix with the chick peas. Heat through in a frying pan for 3–4 minutes, stirring briskly.

3 In a separate pan, heat the butter or ghee and fry the cumin for a few seconds until the fragrance emerges. Add to the vegetables. Add salt to taste.

Spiced Chick Peas
(Masala channa)

SERVES 4
225 g/8 oz chick peas
100 g/4 oz butter or ghee
1 onion, finely chopped
2 cloves garlic, finely chopped
1 tbsp finely grated fresh ginger
225 g/8 oz peeled and chopped
  tomatoes
½ tsp ground coriander
½ tsp chilli powder
1 tbsp mango powder (amchur)
½ tsp ground cumin
1 tsp garam masala
leaves from 1 sprig of coriander
salt

1 Pick over the chick peas, wash thoroughly and soak in water for at least 10 hours. Drain and cook in fresh water for 1–1½ hours, depending on the age of the chick peas, until tender but not soft.

2 Heat the butter or ghee in a pan, add the onion, garlic and ginger and fry until the onion is golden.

3 Add the tomato, coriander, chilli, mango powder, cumin, garam masala and half of the coriander leaves. Cook, stirring briskly to mash the tomato with the back of the spoon into a paste.

4 Drain the chick peas, reserving the cooking liquor, and add to the pan with 2 tbsp of the liquor. Cover and cook over low heat, stirring occasionally, for about 10 minutes, until the chick peas have absorbed the flavours of the spices.

5 Sprinkle on the remaining coriander leaves and add salt to taste.

Right Spiced chick peas/
Masala channa

Soured Chick Peas
(*Chole*)

SERVES 4

200 g/7 oz chick peas, washed
900 ml/1½ pt water
1 teabag
3 tbsp oil
225 g/8 oz potatoes, boiled and
    diced into 1 cm/½ in cubes
2 medium onions, finely chopped
1 clove garlic, crushed
1 cm/½ in ginger, grated
2 tsp ground coriander
2 green chillies, chopped
1½ tbsp mango powder (amchur)
½ tsp chilli powder
¾ tsp salt
175 ml/6 fl oz water
1½ tsp garam masala (see page 13)

1 Soak the chick peas in the water with the teabag overnight.

2 Discard the teabag and place the chick peas and the water in a saucepan and bring to the boil. Cover and simmer for about 1 hour until tender. Drain.

3 Heat the oil in a saucepan over medium heat and fry the diced potatoes until lightly browned. Set aside.

4 In the remaining oil, fry the onions until golden brown. Add the garlic and ginger and fry a further 2 minutes.

5 Add the chick peas, coriander, green chillies, mango powder, chilli, salt and potatoes and stir fry for about 2 minutes until well mixed.

6 Add the water and cook for about 15 minutes. Sprinkle with garam masala. Serve hot with Yoghurt bread (see page 150).

Below Soured chick peas/Chole

Curried Chick Peas
(*Kabli channa*)

SERVES 4
200 g/7 oz chick peas, washed
900 ml/1 ½ pt water
4 tbsp oil
pinch of asafoetida
½ tsp whole cumin seeds
½ tsp ground turmeric
½ tsp chilli powder
I tsp ground coriander
I tsp ground cumin
I ½ tsp mango powder (amchur)
½ tsp salt
2 tbsp lemon juice
I tbsp coriander leaves, chopped
I–2 green chillies, chopped

1 Soak the chick peas in the water overnight.

2 Boil the chick peas with the water, cover and simmer for about 1 hour until tender. Drain and save the liquid.

3 Heat the oil in a large saucepan over medium heat and add the asafoetida and cumin seeds. Let them sizzle for a few seconds.

4 Add the drained chick peas, turmeric, chilli powder, coriander, cumin, mango powder and salt and stir fry for 2–3 minutes.

5 Add 250 ml/8 fl oz of the chick pea stock and cook for 20 minutes, stirring occasionally.

6 Before serving sprinkle with the lemon juice, coriander leaves and green chillies. Serve with Yoghurt bread (see page 150).

Below Curried chick peas/
Kabli channa

Left Curried red kidney beans/
Masala rajma

Curried Red Kidney Beans
(Masala rajma)

SERVES 4

200 g/7 oz red kidney beans, washed
1.2 litres/2 pt water
6 tbsp oil
2 bay leaves
5 cm/2 in cinnamon stick
3 cardamoms
1 large onion, finely sliced
2 cloves garlic, crushed
1 cm/½ in ginger, grated
¾ tsp ground turmeric
½ tsp chilli powder
½ tsp salt
2 tomatoes, chopped
120 ml/4 fl oz water

1 Soak the beans in the water overnight.

2 Boil the beans in the water and then cover and simmer for 1 hour until tender. Drain.

3 Heat the oil in a large saucepan over medium high heat and put in the bay leaves, cinnamon and cardamoms and let them sizzle for a few seconds. Add the onion, garlic and ginger and fry until the onions are golden brown.

4 Add the turmeric, chilli, salt and tomatoes and fry for 1 minute. Add the drained beans and fry with the spices for 2–3 minutes.

5 Add 120 ml/4 fl oz water and bring to the boil, stirring occasionally. Cover, lower heat and cook for 10–15 minutes. Serve with Chappatis (see page 146).

Whole Black Beans
(Mahan ki dal)

SERVES 2

175 g/6 oz whole black beans (sabut urid)
1 cm/½ in ginger, grated
3 dried red chillies
4 cloves garlic, crushed
1½ tsp salt
1.5–1.75 litres/2½–3 pt water
3 tbsp yoghurt, lightly beaten
4 tbsp ghee (see page 21)
1 small onion, chopped
1 tbsp coriander leaves, chopped

1 Wash the beans in several changes of water.

2 Place the beans, ginger, chillies, garlic, salt and water in a large saucepan and bring to a boil. Lower the heat, cover, leaving the lid slightly ajar, and simmer for about 3–3½ hours until the beans are soft. (Add more water if required.)

3 Mash the beans slightly and add the yoghurt and 1 tbsp of the ghee. Cook for a further 30 minutes. (When the beans are cooked they should turn reddish brown in colour and the consistency should be thick.)

4 Heat the remaining ghee and fry the onion until lightly golden. Add this to the hot beans and garnish with the coriander leaves.

The beans could also be boiled in a pressure cooker at 6.75 kg/15 lb weight for 15–20 minutes.

Vegetables

. . . .

India grows a huge variety of vegetables, and combinations of vegetables and spices are endless. Sometimes the spices are used to make a thick sauce, and at other times the vegetables are cooked "dry" (toran) so that the spices stick to them, making a tasty crunchy "crust". Hot spicy vegetables are usually served with rice and mild fragrant ones with bread.

Ripe Mango Curry
(Aam curry)

SERVES 4

4 small sweet ripe mangoes, cubed, with the skins left on

600 ml/1 pt water

2 tsp chilli powder

½ tsp turmeric

salt

grated flesh of ½ coconut

½ tsp ground cumin

6 curry leaves

2 tbsp oil

2 tsp mustard seeds

2 tsp fenugreek seeds

2 red chillies, cut into 4 pieces

2–3 tsp sugar

1 Cook the mango in the water with the chilli powder, turmeric and 1 tsp salt for about 5 minutes, making sure that the mango does not lose its shape.

2 Blend the coconut with the cumin and add to the mango with half the curry leaves.

3 Heat the oil in a frying pan and when hot, add the mustard seeds. Let them sizzle for a few seconds until they have all popped, then add the fenugreek seeds, red chilli and remaining curry leaves. Stir and fry for a few seconds, then add to the mango. Stir well and add sugar and salt to taste.

Extra Thick Buttermilk Curry
(Kalan)

SERVES 4–6

225 g/8 oz yam, peeled and cubed

1 green plantain, peeled and cubed

225 g/8 oz white or red pumpkin, peeled and cubed

½ tsp turmeric

½ tsp chilli powder

grated flesh of 1 small coconut

½ tsp ground cumin

½ tsp ground white pepper

600 ml/1 pt soured buttermilk, made by stirring 3 tbsp water into 225 g/8 oz yoghurt

2 green chillies, cut in half

2 tbsp oil

1 tsp mustard seeds

2 red chillies, cut into 3 or 4 pieces

½ tsp fenugreek seeds

8 curry leaves

2 tbsp sugar

2 tsp salt

1 Cook the yam, plantain and pumpkin in water to cover with the turmeric and chilli powder, over a low heat for about 10 minutes, until tender but not soft.

2 Blend the coconut, cumin and pepper and mix well with the buttermilk, then add to the pan with the vegetables and green chillies. Heat through on a low heat for 3–4 minutes, stirring briskly to prevent the buttermilk from separating.

Left Ripe mango curry/Aam curry

3 Heat the oil in a pan, add the mustard seeds, red chilli, fenugreek seeds and half the curry leaves and let them sizzle for a few seconds, until all the seeds have popped.

4 Stir into the curry with the remaining curry leaves, the sugar and salt to taste.

Stuffed Vegetables
(Sambharia)

SERVES 4
2 long aubergines
6 small potatoes, peeled
6 small onions, peeled
5 green chillies
1 cm/½ in ginger
175 g/6 oz gram flour
1 tbsp ground coriander
½ tsp ground cumin
pinch of ground turmeric
1 tsp salt
¾ tsp sugar
about 120 ml/4 fl oz oil
2 tbsp lime juice
¾ tsp mustard seeds
good pinch of asafoetida
2 tbsp coconut, grated
2 tbsp coriander leaves, chopped

1 Wash the vegetables and dry thoroughly.

2 Cut the aubergine into 4 cm/1½ in slices.

3 Make 2 cuts crosswise on each vegetable; cut about three quarters of the way down the length, but do not cut right through.

4 Grind together 2 green chillies and the ginger to a paste.

5 Make a paste by mixing the gram flour, coriander, cumin, turmeric, salt, sugar, 2½ tbsp oil, lime juice and the chilli and ginger paste.

6 Carefully open the slits in the vegetables and stuff them with this paste. If you have any paste left over after stuffing the vegetables, add it to the vegetables while they are being fried.

7 In a large, heavy-based frying pan, heat the remaining oil, add 3 green chillies, broken in half, mustard and asafoetida and let them sizzle for 8–10 seconds.

8 Add the vegetables carefully, cover and fry over a low heat, occasionally stirring gently. When one side is done, turn the vegetables over, and cover and cook the second side. Add a little more oil if necessary. Serve hot, garnished with the coconut and coriander.

Below Extra thick buttermilk curry/ Kalan

Vegetable Curry with Coconut Milk
(*Sabzi narial*)

SERVES 4
flesh of I coconut, grated
450 g/I lb ripe white pumpkin,
    peeled and cubed
I tbsp coconut oil, mixed with I tbsp
    water
4–6 curry leaves
salt

1 Blend the coconut in a liquidizer with 1 tbsp boiling water. Transfer to a piece of muslin and squeeze out the milk into a bowl. Return the coconut to the liquidizer, add another tbsp boiling water and repeat the process, straining the milk into a separate bowl.

2 Cook the pumpkin in water to cover on a low heat for about 10 minutes until tender, then add the second bowl of coconut milk and bring to the boil. Remove the pan from the heat.

3 Stir in the first bowl of coconut milk, add the coconut oil, curry leaves and salt to taste.

Vegetable Curry with Roasted Coconut
(*Eliseri*)

SERVES 2–3
100 g/4 oz toovar dal
1.2 litres/2 pt water
450 g/I lb red pumpkin, cubed
I tsp chilli powder
½ tsp turmeric
salt
50–75 g/2–3 oz grated or desiccated
    coconut
I tsp ground cumin
6–8 curry leaves
3 tbsp oil
I tsp mustard seeds
2 red chillies, cut into pieces

1 Pick over the dal, wash it thoroughly and cook in the water for about 15 minutes, until you can mash it under the back of a wooden spoon.

2 Meanwhile, cook the pumpkin in water for about 12 minutes, until tender.

3 Drain the dal and the pumpkin, reserving a little of the cooking liquor, and mix the two together with the chilli, turmeric and ½ tsp salt. Cook over a low heat, stirring, for 3–4 minutes, adding a little of the cooking liquor if the mixture threatens to stick. Cover and set aside.

4 Blend half the coconut with the cumin and half the curry leaves. Stir into the curry.

5 Heat the oil in a frying pan and when hot, add the mustard seeds and red chilli. Let them sizzle for a few seconds until all the mustard seeds have popped. Add the remaining grated coconut and curry leaves and fry, stirring briskly, for a few seconds until the fragrance of roasted coconut emerges.

6 Fold the fried spice mixture into the curry and add salt to taste.

Mixed Vegetables
(*Choch chori*)

SERVES 4
I medium potato, peeled
200 g/7 oz white radish, scraped
I smalll aubergine
225 g/8 oz pumpkin, peeled
275 g/10 oz cauliflower stalks
4 tbsp oil
2–3 dried red chillies, broken in half
I tsp panch phoron
2 bay leaves
¾ tsp ground turmeric
½ tsp chilli powder
I½ tsp mustard seeds, ground
I½ tsp salt
½ tsp sugar
½ cup water

1 Cut the potatoes into 8 pieces lengthwise.

2 Quarter the white radish lengthwise and cut into 4 cm/1½ in lengths.

3 Cut off the stalk from the aubergine and quarter lengthwise. Cut into 4 cm/1½ in lengths.

4 Cut the pumpkin into 2.5 cm/ 1 in cubes.

5 Cut the cauliflower stalks into very thin strips of 6 cm/2½ in long.

6 Heat the oil in a karai or saucepan over a medium high heat, add the dried chillies and fry until they become brownish black (about 4–5 seconds).

7 Add the panch phoron and bay leaves and let them sizzle for a few seconds.

8 Add all the vegetables and fry for 3–4 minutes, stirring constantly.

9 Add the turmeric, chilli, mustard, salt and sugar and mix thoroughly with the vegetables.

10 Lower the heat to medium, cover and cook for 10 minutes.

11 Remove the cover, give the vegetables a good stir and then add the water. Bring to the boil, cover again and cook for about 10–15 minutes, until all the vegetables are tender and all the water has evaporated.

Serve with rice and Red lentils with fried onions (see page 39).

Right Vegetables in a yoghurt and coconut sauce/Avial

Vegetables in a Yoghurt and Coconut Sauce
(Avial)

SERVES 4

2 plantains, peeled and cut into
   1 cm/½ in pieces
100 g/4 oz green beans, cut into
   1 cm/½ in pieces
50 g/2 oz carrots, diced into
   5 mm/¼ in cubes
50 g/2 oz peas
¾ tsp chilli powder
½ tsp ground turmeric
¾ tsp salt
350 ml/12 fl oz water
250 ml/8 fl oz unsweetened yoghurt
2 green chillies, chopped
1 tsp ground coriander
2 tbsp desiccated coconut
1 tbsp oil
½ tsp whole mustard seeds
6–8 curry leaves

1 Place the vegetables, chilli powder, turmeric, salt and water in a large saucepan and bring to the boil. Simmer for about 20 minutes until the vegetables are tender. Remove from the heat.

2 Whisk the yoghurt, green chillies, coriander and coconut together and set aside.

3 In a large saucepan heat the oil over medium high heat. Add the mustard seeds and curry leaves, and after 5–6 seconds add the vegetables with the liquid. Cook for 2–3 minutes. Lower the heat and add the yoghurt mixture and, stirring occasionally, cook for a further 4–5 minutes. Serve with rice.

Mixed Vegetable Curry
(Aviyal)

SERVES 4–6

1 plantain, unpeeled
100 g/4 oz runner beans, trimmed
225 g/8 oz yam or potato, peeled
100 g/4 oz white pumpkin or green
   papaya, peeled
½ tsp chilli powder
salt
1 tbsp tamarind juice (see page 22)
2 green chillies
3 tbsp grated coconut
6–8 curry leaves
225 g/8 oz yoghurt
2 tbsp coconut oil
a little sugar, optional

1 Cook the plantain and vegetables in water to cover with the chilli and ½ tsp salt for about 15 minutes, until tender but not soft, stirring occasionally with a wooden spoon. Add the tamarind juice and set aside, covered.

2 Cut the chillies into 4 and crush them with the grated coconut and curry leaves. Stir in the yoghurt and add to the vegetables, mixing well.

3 Mix the coconut oil with a little water to release its fragrance. Pour over the vegetables and add salt to taste. Mix again and add a little sugar, if liked.

Right Mixed vegetable curry/Aviyal

Above Vegetable curry, Kerala style/
Sambar

Vegetable Curry, Kerala Style
(Sambar)

SERVES 4–6
350 g/12 oz toovar dal
1.2 litres/2 pt water
½ tsp turmeric
100–175 g/4–6 oz okra, trimmed
    and cut into 2.5 cm/1 in lengths
3 tbsp oil
1 medium onion, quartered and
    sliced
225 g/8 oz potatoes, cubed
2 tomatoes, peeled and chopped
2 tbsp tamarind juice (see page 22)
75–100 g/3–4 oz grated coconut
4–6 curry leaves
2 tbsp sambar powder (see page 15)
1 tsp mustard seeds
1 red chilli, cut into 4 pieces
salt
coriander leaves, to garnish

1 Pick over the dal, wash it thoroughly and cook in the water with the turmeric for about 15 minutes, until you can mash it under the back of a wooden spoon.

2 Meanwhile, fry the okra in 1 tbsp oil, turning gently, until all the oil is absorbed. This seals the okra and helps it keep its shape. Set aside.

3 When the dal is ready, stir in the onion and potato and continue to cook gently on a low heat for about 8 minutes, until the vegetables are half-cooked.

4 Add the tomato and okra and cook for a further 10 minutes, until the vegetables are tender, adding a little extra water if the pot threatens to boil dry.

5 Stir in the tamarind juice, cover and keep hot.

6 Fry the coconut and half the curry leaves in 1 tbsp oil, then blend with the sambar powder and add to the vegetables.

7 Heat the remaining oil, add the mustard seeds and the red chilli and let them sizzle for a few seconds until all the mustard seeds have popped. Add to the curry.

8 Stir in salt to taste and garnish with coriander leaves.

Vegetable Curry, Tamil Style
(Sambar)

SERVES 4–6
350 g/12 oz toovar dal
1.2 litres/2 pt water
4 drumsticks
1 aubergine
2 medium potatoes
1 medium onion, quartered and
   sliced
½ tsp turmeric
salt
3–4 tbsp tamarind juice
  (see page 22)
3 tbsp sambar powder (see page 15)
1 tomato, cut in 8 pieces
1 tbsp oil
1 tsp mustard seeds
4–6 curry leaves
2 tsp sugar
leaves from 1 sprig of coriander

1 Pick over the dal, wash it thoroughly and cook in the water for about 15 minutes, until you can mash it under the back of a wooden spoon.

2 Meanwhile, scrape the drumsticks and chop into 5cm/2 in lengths. Peel the aubergine and potatoes and cut into cubes, dropping them in a pan of water as you go to prevent discoloration.

3 Add the aubergine, potato and onion to the cooked dal, with a little extra water if necessary, and cook for about 8 minutes, until the vegetables are half-cooked.

4 Add the drumsticks, turmeric and ½ tsp salt, and continue cooking for about 10 minutes, until the vegetables are tender.

5 Stir in the tamarind juice, sambar powder and tomato, cover and keep hot.

6 Heat the oil in a pan and add the mustard seeds and curry leaves. Let them sizzle for a few seconds, until all the mustard seeds have popped, then add to the curry.

7 Stir in sugar and salt to taste and garnish with coriander leaves.

Spicy Mustard Leaves
(Sarson ki saag)

SERVES 4
450 g/1 lb mustard leaves
225 g/8 oz spinach
2–3 green chillies, chopped
1 tsp salt
120 ml/4 fl oz water
about 2 tbsp cornflour
2 tbsp ghee
1 onion, finely chopped
1 cm/½ in ginger, grated
4 cloves garlic, crushed
4 tbsp butter

1 Wash the greens and chop finely

2 Place the greens, chillies, salt and water in a large saucepan and cook on a low heat, stirring occasionally. A lot of water is given out by the greens, but if all the moisture dries up before the greens are cooked, add a little more water. Cook until the greens are tender and all the moisture has evaporated.

3 Place this mixture in a food processor or liquidizer and blend to a purée without adding any more water.

4 After blending, add enough cornflour and mix into the purée to the desired consistency.

5 Heat the ghee in a large frying pan, add the onion, ginger and garlic and fry until lightly golden.

6 Add the puréed greens and, stirring constantly, cook for about 3–4 minutes over a medium heat.

7 Put in a serving dish with the butter on top. Serve with Cornmeal bread (see page 148).

63

Spinach Toran
(*Palak toran*)

SERVES 2
450 g/1 lb fresh spinach
4 tbsp oil
1 small onion, finely chopped
1 green chilli, chopped
75 g/3 oz tomatoes, peeled and
    chopped
75 g/3 oz grated or desiccated
    coconut
salt

1 Wash the spinach, discard any discoloured leaves and tough stalks, and shake dry. Chop as finely as possible and leave in a colander to drain.

2 Heat the oil in a pan and gently fry the onion and green chilli until the onion is transparent.

3 Add the spinach and tomato, cover tightly and cook on a low heat for 4–5 minutes, shaking the pan occasionally, until the spinach has collapsed.

4 Stir in the coconut and add salt to taste.

Photograph on page 54.

Peas and Cauliflower with Ginger
(*Mater gobi*)

SERVES 2
3 tbsp oil
25 g/1 oz ginger, cut into very thin
    strips
1 small cauliflower, broken into large
    florets
225 g/8 oz peas
1 tsp ground turmeric
1 tsp salt
2 tbsp coriander leaves, chopped

1 Heat the oil in a karai or saucepan over a medium high heat. Add the ginger and fry, stirring constantly, until slightly browned.

2 Add the cauliflower, peas, turmeric and salt and mix with the ginger.

3 Lower the heat, cover and, stirring occasionally, cook for about 20–25 minutes until the vegetables are tender.

4 Garnish with the coriander leaves.

Spinach with Lentils and Vegetables
(*Sai bhaji*)

SERVES 2
50 g/2 oz channa dal, washed
600 ml/1 pt water
3 tbsp oil
1 medium onion, finely chopped
1 cm/½ in ginger, grated
2 cloves garlic, crushed
250 g/9 oz spinach, washed and
    chopped
1 medium potato, diced into
    1 cm/½ in cubes
3 tomatoes, chopped
50 g/2 oz peas
½ tsp ground turmeric
½ tsp chilli powder
1 tsp ground coriander
½ tsp salt

1 Bring the dal to the boil in the water over high heat. Cover and simmer for about 40 minutes until the dal is tender. Drain and save the liquid; make it up to 350 ml/ 12 fl oz with water, if necessary.

2 Heat the oil in a large saucepan over medium high heat and fry the onion, ginger and garlic until soft.

3 Add the cooked dal and the rest of the ingredients and stir fry for 2–3 minutes. Add the liquid, cover, lower the heat to medium low and cook for about 30 minutes.

Spinach with Cottage Cheese
(Saag panir)

SERVES 2

4 tbsp oil

175 g/6 oz panir (see page 20),
   drained and cut into 1 cm/½ in
   cubes

1 large onion, finely sliced

4 cloves garlic, crushed

1 cm/½ in ginger, grated

350 g/12 oz frozen spinach, chopped

½ tsp ground turmeric

⅓ tsp chilli powder

1 tsp ground coriander

¾ tsp salt

1 Heat the oil in a karai over medium high heat and fry the panir until brown. Set aside.

2 Add the onion, garlic and ginger to the remaining oil and fry until golden.

3 Add the spinach, turmeric, chilli, coriander and salt and fry for 2–3 minutes.

4 Lower the heat to medium, cover and cook a further 10 minutes.

5 Add the fried panir and, stirring constantly, cook until dry.

Below Spinach with cottage cheese/
Saag panir

65

Cabbage with Peas
(*Bund gobi aur mater*)

SERVES 4
3 tbsp oil
2 bay leaves
¾ tsp whole cumin seeds
700 g/1 ½ lb cabbage, finely
    shredded
1 tsp ground turmeric
½ tsp chilli powder
1 ½ tsp ground cumin
1 tsp ground coriander
2 tomatoes, chopped
¾ tsp salt
½ tsp sugar
100 g/4 oz peas

1 Heat the oil in a karai over medium high heat and add the bay leaves and the cumin seeds. Let them sizzle for a few seconds.

2 Add the cabbage and stir for 2–3 minutes.

3 Add the turmeric, chilli, cumin, coriander, tomatoes, salt and sugar and mix with the cabbage.

4 Lower the heat, cover and cook for 15 minutes. Add the peas and cover again. Continue to cook for a further 15 minutes, stirring occasionally.

5 Remove the cover, turn the heat up to medium high and, stirring continuously, cook until it is dry.

Below Cabbage with peas/
Bund gobi aur mater

Cottage Cheese with Peas
(*Mater panir*)

SERVES 4
6 tbsp oil
275 g/10 oz panir (see page 20),
    drained and cut into 1 cm/½ in
    pieces
6 tbsp onion mixture (see page 22)
1 tsp ground turmeric
½ tsp chilli powder
1 tsp ground coriander
¾ tsp salt
175 g/6 oz peas
250 ml/8 fl oz water
1 tbsp coriander leaves, chopped
    (optional)

1 Heat the oil in a karai over medium high heat and fry the panir pieces until golden brown. Remove and drain on paper towels.

2 In the remaining oil add the onion mixture and fry for 3 minutes, stirring constantly. Add the turmeric, chilli, coriander and salt and continue to fry for a further 2–3 minutes.

3 Add the peas and mix thoroughly. Add the water and bring to the boil. Cover, lower heat to medium low and simmer for 5 minutes. Gently add the pieces of fried panir and simmer a further 10 minutes. Garnish with the coriander leaves and serve hot.

Right Cottage cheese with peas/ Mater panir

Left Dry peas/Sukha mater

Dry Peas
(*Sukha mater*)

SERVES 4
2 tbsp oil
5 cm/2 in ginger, cut into very thin
    strips
700 g/1 ½ lb peas (fresh or frozen)
1 tsp salt
½ tsp mango powder (amchur)

1 Heat the oil in a karai or saucepan over a medium high heat and fry the ginger, stirring constantly, until slightly browned.

2 Add the peas and salt and mix with the ginger.

3 Lower the heat, cover and cook for about 15 minutes until the peas are tender.

4 Add the mango powder, mix and remove from the heat.

Cabbage with Coconut
(*Bund gobi aur narial*)

SERVES 4
2 tbsp oil
2 bay leaves
¾ tsp whole cumin seeds
1–2 green chillies, chopped
700 g/1½ lb cabbage, shredded
¾ tsp salt
⅓ tsp sugar
3 tbsp desiccated coconut
½ tsp ground cumin

1 Heat the oil in a karai over medium high heat and add the bay leaves, cumin seeds and the green chillies and let them sizzle for a few seconds.

2 Add the cabbage, salt and sugar and mix. Cover, lower the heat to medium and cook for about 15 minutes until half done.

3 Add the coconut and ground cumin and fry, stirring constantly for 10–15 minutes until all the moisture has evaporated.

Below Cabbage with coconut/ Bund gobi aur narial

Dry Spiced Cabbage
(*Gobi bhaji*)

SERVES 4
450 g/1 lb cabbage
225 g/8 oz potatoes
2 tbsp oil
½ tsp ground cumin
½ tsp ground coriander
½ tsp turmeric
¼ tsp asafoetida
½ tsp chilli powder
salt

1 Cut the cabbage into strips, and peel and finely chop the potatoes.

2 Heat the oil and fry the cumin, coriander, turmeric, asafoetida and chilli for 3–4 minutes, until the fragrance of the spices emerges.

3 Add the cabbage and potato, sprinkle on 1–2 tbsp water and ½ tsp salt, cover the pan tightly and cook on a low heat for 5–6 minutes, until the potato is cooked.

4 Take the pot off the heat and let it stand, covered, for 3–4 minutes. Add extra salt to taste.

Cabbage Toran
(*Gobi toran*)

SERVES 2
2 tbsp oil
1–2 tsp polished split black lentils
    (urid dal)
½ tsp mustard seeds
4–6 curry leaves
1 small onion, finely chopped
1 green chilli, sliced
15 g/½ oz fresh ginger, finely grated
450 g/1 lb cabbage, very finely
    chopped or grated
½ tsp turmeric
50–75 g/2–3 oz grated coconut
salt

1 Heat the oil in a large pan, big enough to hold the cabbage. Add the dal and fry until golden.

2 Add the mustard seeds and let them sizzle for a few seconds until they have all popped.

3 Add the curry leaves, onion, green chilli and ginger and continue to fry, stirring, for 3–4 minutes.

4 Stir the cabbage into the pan with the turmeric, cover tightly and cook for about 4 minutes on a low heat until tender but not soft.

5 Stir in the grated coconut and add salt to taste.

Above Dry spiced cabbage/
Gobi bhaji

Red Peppers Stuffed with Vegetables
(*Lal mirchi sabzi*)

SERVES 4
175 g/6 oz potatoes
50–75 g/2–3 oz butter or ghee
1 small onion, finely chopped
15 g/½ oz fresh ginger, finely grated
1 clove garlic, finely chopped
100 g/4 oz tomatoes, peeled and
    chopped
½ tsp turmeric
½ tsp chilli powder
salt
½ tsp ground coriander
½ tsp garam masala
leaves from 1 sprig of coriander
4 large red peppers
2 tbsp oil

1 Peel the potatoes, dice them and leave in a pan of cold water to prevent discoloration.

2 Heat the butter or ghee in a pan, add the onion, ginger and garlic and fry until the onion is golden.

3 Add the tomato, turmeric, chilli powder, ½ tsp salt and ground coriander, cook and stir briskly, squashing the tomato under the back of a wooden spoon to make a thick paste.

4 Drain the potato and add to the spice mix with 2–4 tbsp water. Cover and cook on a low heat, stirring occasionally, for 10–15 minutes, until the potato is tender but not soft.

5 Add the garam masala and coriander leaves. Cook for a further

3–4 minutes, then set aside, covered.

6 Wash the peppers and, with a sharp knife, cut off the top, which can be used as a lid. Scrape them out and discard the seeds and pith.

7 Stuff the peppers with the potato curry and replace the lids.

Above Red peppers stuffed with vegetables/Lal mirchi sabzi

8 Heat the oil in a pan, put in the peppers and fry gently on all sides until cooked, about 15 minutes. Alternatively, stand the peppers in a greased dish, cover and cook in the oven at 200°C/400°F/Gas 6 for 30 minutes, until tender.

Green Peppers Stuffed with Meat
(*Mirchi gosht*)

SERVES 4
100 g/4 oz potato
100 g/4 oz butter or ghee
1 small onion, finely chopped
15 g/½ oz fresh ginger, finely grated
2 cloves garlic, finely chopped
100 g/4 oz tomatoes, roughly
   chopped
½ tsp turmeric
1 tsp ground coriander
½ tsp garam masala
½ tsp fennel seeds
leaves from 1 sprig of coriander
½ tsp chilli powder
225 g/8 oz lean minced meat (beef
   or lamb)
1 tsp lemon juice
salt
4 large green peppers
2 tbsp oil

1 Peel the potato, dice and leave in a pan of cold water to prevent discoloration.

2 Heat the butter or ghee in a pan, add the onion, ginger and garlic and fry until the onion is golden.

3 Add the tomato, turmeric, ground coriander, garam masala, fennel seeds, half the coriander leaves and the chilli powder and continue to fry for a few minutes until the fat runs clear of the spices.

4 Drain the potato and stir into the pan with the minced meat. Cook for 10–15 minutes, stirring occasionally, until cooked through.

5 Sprinkle on the lemon juice, add salt to taste and take off the heat.

6 Wash the peppers and with a sharp knife, cut off the top, which can be used as a lid. Scrape them out and discard the seeds and pith.

7 Stuff the peppers with the curry and replace the lids.

8 Heat the oil in a pan, put in the peppers and fry gently on all sides until cooked, about 15 minutes. Alternatively, stand the peppers in a greased dish, cover and cook in the oven at 200°C/400°F/Gas 6 for 30 minutes, until tender.

Carrot Toran
(*Gajar toran*)

SERVES 2
50 g/2 oz toovar dal
225 g/8 oz carrots, peeled and diced
salt
2 tbsp oil
1 tsp mustard seeds
4 curry leaves
1 or 2 green chillies, seeded and
   sliced
75 g/3 oz grated or desiccated
   coconut

1 Pick over the dal, wash thoroughly and cook in water to cover for 15 minutes, until it can be crushed under the back of a wooden spoon and almost all the water has been absorbed.

2 Cook the carrots in salted water to cover for 10 minutes, until just tender. Drain and add to the dal.

3 Heat the oil in a pan and when hot, add the mustard seeds, curry leaves and chilli. Let them sizzle for a few seconds until all the seeds have popped, then add to the carrots.

4 Stir in the coconut and heat through over a low flame for 2–3 minutes, stirring, until the curry is quite dry. Add salt to taste.

Green Papaya Toran
(*Papaya toran*)

SERVES 2
450 g/1 lb unripe green papaya,
   peeled and cubed
salt
2 tbsp oil
2 tsp polished split black lentils
   (urid dal)
1 small onion, finely chopped
1 tsp mustard seeds
4–6 curry leaves
1 red chilli, cut into 4 or 6 pieces
100 g/4 oz grated or desiccated
   coconut

1 Cook the papaya in salted water to cover for 10–15 minutes, until tender but not soft. Drain and keep hot.

2 Heat the oil in a frying pan and add the dal, onion, mustard seeds, curry leaves and red chilli. Fry until the onion is golden, then add the papaya, stir and fry for 3–4 minutes.

3 Stir in the grated coconut and add salt to taste.

Green Beans Toran I
(*Hari moong toran*)

SERVES 2
1 tbsp oil
1 tsp mustard seeds
1 red chilli, cut into 4 or 6 pieces
4–6 curry leaves
1 small onion, finely chopped
225 g/8 oz green beans, trimmed and
     cut into 2.5 cm/1 in lengths
salt
50–75 g/2–3 oz grated coconut

1 Heat the oil in a heavy-based saucepan and when hot, add the mustard seeds. Let them sizzle for a few seconds until they have all popped.

2 Add the red chilli, curry leaves and onion and fry gently, stirring, until the onion is golden.

3 Turn the heat to low and add the beans, 1 tbsp water, ½ tsp salt and the coconut. Cook, with the lid firmly on, for about 10 minutes, until the beans are tender but not soft, stirring occasionally.

4 Let the pot stand for about 5 minutes and add extra salt if necessary before serving.

Green Beans Toran II
(*Hari moong toran*)

SERVES 2
1 or 2 green chillies, chopped
75 g/3 oz grated coconut
4–6 curry leaves
1 clove garlic, chopped
225 g/8 oz green beans, trimmed and
     cut into 2.5 cm/1 in lengths
½ tsp turmeric
2 tbsp oil
2 tsp polished split black lentils
     (urid dal)
1 tsp mustard seeds
salt

1 Crush the green chilli with the coconut, curry leaves and garlic and mix with the green beans and turmeric in a heavy-based saucepan. Add 1–2 tbsp water and cook over a very low heat, covered tightly, for 10–15 minutes, until tender. Stir occasionally to prevent sticking.

2 Heat the oil in a pan, add the dal and fry until golden.

3 Add the mustard seeds and let them sizzle for a few seconds until they have all popped. Add to the beans and cook for a further 3–4 minutes.

4 Let the pot stand off the heat, covered, for 3–4 minutes, then add salt to taste.

Above Beans with coconut/
Sukhi bean aur narial

Beans with Coconut
(*Sukhi bean aur narial*)

SERVES 4
3 tbsp oil
½ tsp kalonji
2–3 dried red chillies
450 g/1 lb green beans washed and
    cut into 2.5 cm/1 in lengths
2 tbsp desiccated coconut
½ tsp salt

1 Heat the oil in a karai over medium high heat, add the kalonji and chillies and let them sizzle for a few seconds.

2 Add the beans and stir fry for 10 minutes.

3 Add the coconut and salt and mix in thoroughly with the beans, and stirring constantly to avoid sticking cook a further 5–7 minutes. Serve with Poori (see page 152).

Panir Bhiyia

SERVES 2
2 tbsp oil
1 medium onion, finely chopped
1 clove garlic, crushed
275 g/10 oz panir (see page 20),
    drained
½ tsp ground turmeric
½ tsp salt
1 small green pepper, seeded and
    cut into 1 cm/½ in pieces
1 large tomato, chopped
1–2 green chillies, chopped
1 tbsp coriander leaves, chopped

1 Heat the oil in a karai over medium heat and fry the onion and garlic for 5 minutes.

2 Add the panir, turmeric and salt and stir fry for 5 minutes.

3 Add the green pepper and tomato and cook for 8–10 minutes, stirring occasionally.

4 Sprinkle with the green chillies and coriander leaves and remove from the heat. Serve with Poori (see page 152).

Left Panir bhiyia

Potatoes with Fenugreek Leaves
(*Aloo methi*)

SERVES 2
450 g/1 lb potatoes
handful fresh fenugreek leaves or 1
   tbsp dried fenugreek leaves
3 tbsp ghee (see page 21)
½ tsp ground turmeric
1 tsp ground cumin
½ tsp chilli powder
1 tsp salt

1 Wash the potatoes and then peel and cut them into 2 cm/¾ in cubes.

2 If you are using fresh fenugreek, remove the tough lower stalk, wash the leaves thoroughly and chop finely. If you are using dried fenugreek, soak it in water for about 20–25 minutes, gently squeeze the water out and chop the leaves. Remove any tough stalks.

3 Heat the ghee in a large frying pan. Add the potatoes and, stirring constantly, fry for about 3–4 minutes.

4 Add the turmeric, cumin, chilli and salt and mix with the potatoes and cook for a further minute.

5 Add the fenugreek leaves and mix with the potatoes. Lower the heat, cover and, stirring occasionally, cook for about 20 minutes until the potatoes are tender. Add 1–2 tbsp of water if necessary.

Potato and Green Papaya Curry
(*Aloo peper dalna*)

SERVES 4
6 tbsp oil
450 g/1 lb green papaya, peeled,
   seeded and cut into 2.5 cm/1 in
   cubes
450 g/1 lb potatoes, peeled and cut
   into 2.5 cm/1 in cubes
1 tsp whole cumin seeds
2 bay leaves
2 tomatoes, chopped
¾ tsp ground turmeric
½ tsp chilli powder
1½ tsp ground cumin
¾ tsp salt
large pinch of sugar
300 ml/½ pt water
2 tsp ghee (see page 21)
½ tsp garam masala powder

1 Heat the oil in a karai or a saucepan over a medium high heat.

2 Fry the papaya, a few pieces at a time, until slightly brown. Remove and set aside.

3 Fry the potatoes, a few pieces at a time, until slightly brown. Remove and set aside.

4 Lower the heat to medium, add the cumin seeds and bay leaves and let them sizzle for 3–4 seconds. Add the tomatoes and fry for 1–2 minutes.

5 Add the turmeric, chilli, cumin, salt and sugar and mix with the tomatoes and fry for a further 1 minute.

6 Add the papaya and potatoes and mix well with the spices. Add the water and bring to a boil. Cover and cook for 15–20 minutes until the vegetables are tender.

7 Add the ghee and the garam masala before removing from the heat.

Right Potatoes with fenugreek leaves/Aloo methi

Potato Masala Curry
(*Aloo masala*)

SERVES 4

3 or 4 medium potatoes, cubed
1 large onion, finely chopped
½ tsp turmeric
salt
2 green chillies, chopped
2 tsp garam masala
2 tbsp grated or desiccated coconut
15 g/½ oz fresh ginger, finely grated
2 tbsp oil
1 tsp mustard seeds
4–6 curry leaves
leaves from 1 sprig of coriander

1 Cook the potato in just enough water to cover with three-quarters of the onion, the turmeric, ½ tsp salt and the green chilli, for about 8 minutes, until half-cooked.

2 Meanwhile, blend the garam masala, coconut and ginger in a liquidizer. Add to the potato and continue to cook for a further 8 minutes, until tender but not soft.

3 Heat the oil in a frying pan and add the mustard seeds. Let them sizzle for a few seconds until they have all popped, then add the remaining chopped onion and fry until golden. Stir into the curry.

4 Add salt to taste and sprinkle on the curry and coriander leaves.

Right Potato masala curry/
Aloo masala

Potatoes with Poppy Seeds
(*Aloo posto*)

SERVES 2
3 tbsp oil
450 g/1 lb potatoes, diced into
    2 cm/¾ in pieces
2 tbsp poppy seeds, ground
1 tbsp desiccated coconut
¾ tsp salt
a big pinch of sugar
2–3 green chillies, chopped

1 Heat the oil in a karai over medium heat and fry the potatoes, stirring occasionally until nearly done, about 15 minutes.

2 Add the poppy seeds, coconut, salt, sugar and green chillies and continue cooking until the potatoes are tender. Serve with rice.

Potatoes with Tamarind
(*Imlee aloo*)

SERVES 4
6 tbsp oil
1 tsp whole cumin seeds
2 large onions, finely chopped
4 cloves garlic, crushed
700 g/1½ lb small potatoes, peeled
    and boiled
1 cm/½ in ginger, grated
½ tsp ground turmeric
¼ tsp chilli powder
¾ tsp salt
1 tsp sugar
75 ml/3 fl oz thick tamarind juice
    (see page 22)
½ tsp roasted ground cumin
    (see page 23)

1 Heat the oil in a karai over medium high heat, add the cumin seeds and let them sizzle for a few seconds.

2 Add the onions and garlic and fry them until the onions are soft.

3 Lower the heat to medium low, add the potatoes and grated ginger and fry for 5–7 minutes, stirring occasionally.

4 Add the turmeric, chilli, salt, sugar and tamarind juice and cook for 10–15 minutes.

5 Before removing from the heat, sprinkle with the roasted ground cumin.

Ripe Plantain Curry with Yoghurt
(*Kela dahi*)

SERVES 4
2 or 3 ripe plantains, peeled and
    thickly sliced
600 ml/1 pt water
½ tsp chilli powder
½ tsp turmeric
4–6 tbsp grated or desiccated
    coconut
½ tsp cumin seeds or ground cumin
225 g/8 oz yoghurt
2 tbsp oil
1 tsp mustard seeds
1 red chilli, cut into 3 or 4 pieces
6–8 curry leaves
2–3 tbsp brown sugar
salt

1 Cook the plantain in the water with the chilli powder and turmeric for 5 minutes, until tender but not soft, and most of the water has evaporated.

2 Grind or pound the coconut with the cumin (or blend in a liquidizer), then mix with the yoghurt.

3 Stir the yoghurt into the plantain over a low heat. Cook for 3–4 minutes to heat through, stirring all the time to prevent the yoghurt from separating. Cover and set aside.

4 Heat the oil in a pan and when hot, add the mustard seeds. Let them sizzle for a few seconds until they have all popped, then add the red chilli and half the curry leaves. Continue to fry for a few seconds, then add to the curry.

5 Stir in sugar and salt to taste and sprinkle with the remaining curry leaves.

Right Potatoes with green peppers and coconut/Aloo aur capsicum

Potatoes with Green Peppers and Coconut
(Aloo aur capsicum)

SERVES 2
3 tbsp oil
½ tsp whole mustard seeds
pinch of asafoetida
6–8 curry leaves
450 g/1 lb potatoes, boiled, peeled
    and diced into 1 cm/½ in cubes
1 green pepper, seeded and cut into
    1 cm/½ in pieces
3 tbsp desiccated coconut
½ tsp salt
2 green chillies, chopped
1 tbsp coriander leaves, chopped

1 Heat the oil in a karai over medium heat, add the mustard seeds, asafoetida and curry leaves and let them sizzle for 3–4 seconds.

2 Add the potatoes and green pepper and stir fry for 5 minutes.

3 Add the coconut and salt and, stirring occasionally, cook for another 5–7 minutes.

4 Before removing from the heat, sprinkle with the chillies and coriander leaves. Serve hot with Poori (see page 152).

Spicy Potatoes
(*Rasadar aloo*)

SERVES 2–3
700 g/1½ lb small potatoes
2–3 medium tomatoes
4 tbsp oil
1 tsp cumin seeds
pinch of asafoetida
¾ tsp ground turmeric
1 tsp ground coriander
¾ tsp chilli powder
1 tsp paprika
1 tsp salt
300 ml/½ pt water
½ tsp garam masala
2 tbsp coriander leaves, chopped

1 Peel the potatoes and wash them.

2 Place the tomatoes in boiling water for 10 seconds. Carefully peel and chop them.

3 Heat the oil over a medium high heat in a karai or saucepan. Add the cumin seeds and asafoetida and let them sizzle for 5–6 seconds.

4 Add the chopped tomatoes, turmeric, coriander, chilli, paprika and salt and, stirring constantly, fry for 30 seconds. (If it starts to stick to the bottom, sprinkle on a little water.)

5 Add the potatoes and fry for 2–3 minutes, stirring constantly.

6 Add the water and bring to a boil. Lower the heat, cover and cook for about 15 minutes until the potatoes are tender.

7 Add the garam masala and mix.

8 Remove and garnish with the coriander leaves.

Dry potatoes
(*Sukha aloo*)

SERVES 2–3
700 g/1½ lb potatoes, washed
4 tbsp oil
1 tsp cumin seeds
pinch of asafoetida
¾ tsp ground turmeric
¾ tsp chilli powder
1 tsp ground coriander
1 tsp mango powder (amchur)
1 tsp salt

1 Boil the potatoes with the skins still on. Peel and cut into large pieces (take care you do not over-cook them).

2 Heat the oil in a karai or saucepan over a medium high heat. Add the cumin seeds and asafoetida and let them sizzle for about 5–6 seconds.

3 Add the turmeric, chilli, coriander, mango powder and salt and fry for 5–7 seconds. If it starts to stick, sprinkle a little water on the mixture.

4 Add the potatoes and, stirring gently, fry for 5 minutes.

Above Spicy potatoes/Rasadar aloo

Right Dry potatoes/Sukha aloo

Cauliflower with Potato and Tomatoes
(*Aloo gobi tamatar masala*)

SERVES 4
75 g/3 oz potato
450 g/1 lb cauliflower
50 g/2 oz butter or ghee
1 small onion, finely chopped
15 g/½ oz fresh ginger, finely grated
1 clove garlic, finely chopped
2 green chillies, cut into 4–6 pieces
leaves from 1 sprig of coriander
100 g/4 oz tomatoes, peeled and
    roughly chopped
½ tsp chilli powder
½ tsp turmeric
½ tsp ground coriander
½ tsp fennel seeds
½ tsp garam masala
1 tsp ground cumin
salt

1 Peel the potato and cut into chunks. Divide the cauliflower into florets, discarding the tough stalks. Put the vegetables in a pan of cold water to prevent discoloration.

2 Heat three-quarters of the butter or ghee in a heavy-based pan and add the onion, ginger, garlic, green chilli and half the coriander leaves. Stir and fry until the onion is golden.

3 Stir in the tomato, add the chilli powder, turmeric, coriander, fennel seeds, garam masala and half the cumin and cook over a low heat, squashing the tomato under the back of a wooden spoon to make a thick paste.

4 Drain and add the vegetables with about 4 tbsp water. Cover and cook for 15 minutes, until the potato is tender but not soft.

5 Meanwhile, heat the remaining butter or ghee in a separate pan and add the remaining cumin. Add to the curry with the remaining coriander leaves and salt to taste.

Above Cauliflower with potatoes and tomatoes/Aloo gobi tamatar masala

Cauliflower with Coconut and Spices
(*Narial phul gobi masala*)

SERVES 4
75 g/3 oz potato
450 g/1 lb cauliflower
100 g/4 oz grated coconut
1 green chilli
15 g/½ oz fresh ginger, finely grated
1 clove garlic, finely chopped
leaves from 1 sprig of coriander
½ tsp turmeric
1 small onion, finely chopped
4 cashew nuts
2 tbsp oil
1 tsp mustard seeds
4–6 curry leaves
1 red chilli, cut into 4 pieces
75 g/3 oz tomatoes, chopped
2 tsp lemon juice
salt

1 Peel the potato and cut into chunks. Divide the cauliflower into florets, discarding the tough stalks. Put the vegetables in a pan of cold water to prevent discoloration.

2 In a liquidizer, coarsely blend the coconut, green chilli, ginger, garlic, coriander leaves, turmeric, onion and cashew nuts.

3 Drain the vegetables, turn them in the spice mixture to coat and leave for about 10 minutes to absorb the flavours.

4 Heat the oil in a pan and when hot, add the mustard seeds, half the curry leaves and the red chilli. Leave them to sizzle for a few seconds until all the seeds have popped.

5 Add the spiced vegetables and tomatoes to the pan, cover and cook on a low heat, stirring occasionally, for about 10 minutes, until the potato is tender but not soft.

6 Sprinkle over the lemon juice, stir in the remaining curry leaves and add salt to taste.

Green Beans and Potato Toran
(*Aloo hari moong toran*)

SERVES 2
50–75 g/2–3 oz butter or ghee
1 small onion, finely chopped
225 g/8 oz tomatoes, peeled and
　finely chopped
½ tsp garam masala
½ tsp turmeric
½ tsp chilli powder
225 g/8 oz green beans, trimmed and
　cut into 2.5 cm/1 in lengths
225 g/8 oz potatoes, peeled and
　diced
1 green chilli, cut into pieces
15 g/½ oz fresh ginger, finely grated
1 clove garlic, finely chopped
leaves from 1 sprig of coriander
salt

1 Heat the butter or ghee in a large saucepan and fry the onion until golden.

2 Add the tomato, stir well and squash it with the back of a wooden spoon until it forms a paste.

3 Add the garam masala, turmeric and chilli powder and continue to fry, stirring, for about 5 minutes.

4 Add the beans, potatoes, green chilli, ginger, garlic and coriander leaves with 1 tbsp water and cook gently over a low heat, with the lid tightly on, stirring occasionally, for 10–15 minutes, until the vegetables are done. Add salt to taste.

Mushroom with Potatoes and Onions
(*Khumbi, aloo aur pyaz*)

SERVES 2
5 tbsp oil
I large potato, diced into 2 cm/¾ in pieces
4 cardamoms
4 cm/1½ in cinnamon stick
2 bay leaves
I large onion, finely sliced
2 cloves garlic, crushed
2 cm/¾ in ginger, grated
I tsp ground turmeric
½ tsp chilli powder
½ tsp salt
a big pinch of sugar

I½ tsp white vinegar
225 g/8 oz mushrooms, quartered

1 Heat the oil in a karai over medium high heat. Add the potatoes and fry for 2–3 minutes until light golden in colour. Remove the potatoes and set aside.

2 To the same oil add the cardamoms, cinnamon and bay leaves and let them sizzle for a few seconds.

3 Add the onions, garlic and ginger and fry for 4--5 minutes until soft and golden.

Above Mushrooms with potatoes and onions/Khumbi aloo

4 Add the turmeric, chilli, salt, sugar and vinegar and fry, stirring continuously, for another minute.

5 Add the mushrooms and potatoes to the spice mixture and mix thoroughly.

6 Lower the heat to medium, cover and cook for about 15 minutes until the potatoes are tender.

Opposite Green beans and potato toran/Aloo hari moong

83

Roasted Cauliflower
(*Baked gobi*)

SERVES 2
4 medium tomatoes
1 large onion
3 cloves garlic
1 cm/½ in ginger
2 tbsp ghee (see page 21)
¾ tsp ground turmeric
½ tsp chilli powder
½ tsp garam masala (see page 13)
175 g/6 oz peas
½ tsp salt
1 medium-sized cauliflower,
   blanched

1 Blend the tomatoes, onion, garlic and ginger in a blender until you have a paste.

2 Heat the ghee in a frying pan over medium heat and add the paste, turmeric, chilli and garam masala and stir fry until the ghee and spices separate, about 5–6 minutes.

3 Add the peas and salt and cook a further 5 minutes, stirring constantly. Remove from the heat.

4 Place the cauliflower in a large oven-proof dish and pour the spices over it. Place in a preheated oven at 190°C/375°F/Gas 5 for 30–35 minutes. Serve on a flat plate with the peas and spices poured over.

Opposite Dry potato and cauliflower/Aloo gobi chokka

Below Roasted cauliflower/ Baked gobi

Dry Potato and Cauliflower
(*Aloo gobi chokka*)

SERVES 4
3 tbsp oil
¾ tsp kalonji
3–4 green chillies, split in half
1 small cauliflower, cut into
    2 cm/¾ in pieces
450 g/1 lb potatoes, diced into
    2 cm/¾ in pieces
¾ tsp salt

1 Heat the oil in a karai over medium high heat and add the kalonji and green chillies. Let them sizzle for a few seconds.

2 Add the cauliflower and potatoes and stir for 1–2 minutes.

3 Lower the heat to medium low, cover and cook for 15–20 minutes, stirring occasionally.

4 Add the salt, turn up the heat and, stirring constantly, fry until the vegetables are tender. Serve with Lucchis (see page 148).

Cauliflower with Coconut Milk
(*Narial phul gobi*)

SERVES 4
flesh of 1 coconut, grated
450 g/1 lb cauliflower, cut into
    florets, tough stalks discarded
100 g/4 oz potatoes, peeled and
    cubed
15 g/½ oz fresh ginger, finely grated
½ tsp turmeric
½ tsp sambar powder (see page 15)
1 small onion, finely chopped
1 green chilli, sliced
4–6 curry leaves
2–3 tbsp oil
1 tsp mustard seeds
salt
leaves from 1 sprig of coriander

1 Blend the coconut in a liquidizer with 1 tbsp boiling water. Transfer to a sheet of muslin and squeeze the milk into a bowl. Return the coconut to the liquidizer and repeat the process.

2 Simmer the cauliflower and potato in the coconut milk with the ginger, turmeric, sambar powder, three-quarters of the onion and the chilli for about 12 minutes, until the vegetables are tender but not soft. Add the curry leaves.

3 Meanwhile, heat the oil in a pan and when hot, add the mustard seeds. Let them sizzle for a few seconds until they have all popped.

4 Add the remaining onion and fry until golden, then add to the curry.

5 Add salt to taste and garnish with coriander leaves.

Cauliflower and Potato Curry
(*Aloo gobi dalna*)

SERVES 4

6 tbsp oil
450 g/1 lb potatoes, peeled and
    quartered
1 small cauliflower, cut into large
    florets
pinch of asafoetida
¾ tsp ground turmeric
½ tsp chilli powder
1½ tsp ground cumin
¾ tsp salt
big pinch of sugar
2 tomatoes, chopped
300 ml/1 pt water
2 tsp ghee (see page 21)
½ tsp garam masala (see page 13)

1 Heat the oil in a karai over medium high heat.

2 Fry the potatoes a few pieces at a time until slightly brown. Remove and set aside.

3 Fry the cauliflower pieces a few at a time until brown spots appear on them. Remove and set aside.

4 Lower the heat to medium, add the asafoetida and after 3–4 seconds add the turmeric, chilli, cumin, salt and sugar. Mix the spices together, add the tomatoes and fry for 1 minute with the spices.

5 Add the water and bring to the boil. Put in the potatoes, cover and cook for 10 minutes.

6 Add the cauliflower, cover again and cook a further 5–7 minutes until the potatoes and cauliflower are tender.

7 Add the ghee and sprinkle with the garam masala. Remove from the heat and serve hot with rice and red lentils.

Below Cauliflower and potato curry/Aloo gobi dalna

Above Cauliflower with potatoes
and peas/Aloo gobi aur mater

Cauliflower with Potatoes and Peas
(*Aloo gobi aur mater*)

SERVES 4

4 tbsp oil

2 medium onions, finely chopped

450 g/1 lb potatoes, diced into
2 cm/¾ in pieces

1 small cauliflower, cut into
2 cm/¾ in pieces

½ tsp ground turmeric

⅓ tsp chilli powder

1 tsp ground cumin

2 tomatoes, chopped

1 tsp salt

¼ tsp sugar

200 g/7 oz peas

½ tsp garam masala (see page 13)

1 Heat the oil in a karai over medium high heat.

2 Add the onions and fry for 3–4 minutes until light brown.

3 Add the potatoes and cauliflower and stir. Add the turmeric, chilli, cumin, tomatoes, salt and sugar. Stir and fry for 2–3 minutes.

4 Add the peas, cover and reduce heat to medium low and cook for about 20 minutes until the potatoes and cauliflower are tender. During the cooking period stir the vegetables a few times to stop them sticking.

5 Sprinkle with garam masala before serving.

Pumpkin with Spices
(*Masala kaddu*)

SERVES 2
2 tbsp oil
½ tsp kalonji
2 dried red chillies
1 large onion, finely sliced
450 g/1 lb pumpkin, diced into
    1 cm/½ in cubes
½ tsp ground turmeric
½ tsp chilli powder
½ tsp salt

1 Heat oil in a karai over medium high heat, add the kalonji and red chillies and let them sizzle for about 15 seconds. Add the onions and fry until golden.

2 Add the pumpkin, turmeric, chilli and salt and stir fry for 2–3 minutes. Cover, lower heat to medium and cook a further 10 minutes. Serve hot with Lucchi (see page 148).

Pumpkin and Potato Curry
(*Aloo pethi*)

SERVES 2
1 tbsp sambar powder (see page 15)
225 g/8 oz unripe red pumpkin, peeled and cubed
100 g/4 oz potato, peeled and cubed
2 tbsp oil
½ tsp mustard seeds
1 small onion, chopped

4–6 curry leaves
¼ tsp asafoetida
½ tsp turmeric
1 red chilli
100 g/4 oz tomatoes, peeled and chopped
salt

1 Sprinkle the sambar powder over the potato and pumpkin. Stir well to coat and leave aside.

2 Heat the oil in a pan and add the mustard seeds. Let them sizzle for a few seconds until they have all popped, then add the onions, curry leaves, asafoetida, turmeric and red chilli. Stir well and fry until the onion is golden.

3 Add the marinated vegetables, the tomato and enough water to just cover and simmer for about 15 minutes over a low heat, until the vegetables are tender but not soft and the sauce is thick. Add salt to taste.

Left Pumpkin with spices/
Masala kaddu

Dry Doddy
(Lau ghonto)

SERVES 2–3
2 tbsp ghee
¾ tsp whole cumin seeds
2 bay leaves
700 g/1½ lb doddy, peeled and
    grated
½ tsp salt
pinch of sugar
½ tbsp coriander leaves, chopped

1 Heat the ghee in a karai over medium heat and add the cumin seeds and bay leaves and let them sizzle for a few seconds. Add the doddy and fry for 3–4 minutes, stirring constantly.

2 Cover, lower heat and cook for 20–25 minutes, stirring so that it does not stick to the bottom.

Above Dry doddy/Lau ghonto

3 Remove the cover, turn the heat up to medium high, add the salt and sugar and, stirring constantly, fry until the doddy is browned and dry.

4 Serve hot, sprinkled with the chopped coriander leaves.

Aubergine and Potato Toran
(*Baigan aloo toran*)

SERVES 4
300 g/10 oz small aubergines
225 g/8 oz potatoes
15 g/½ oz fresh ginger, finely grated
2 cloves garlic, chopped
leaves from 1 sprig of coriander
1 tsp ground coriander
½ tsp chilli powder
½ tsp garam masala
½ tsp turmeric
juice from 25–50 g/1–2 oz seedless
    tamarind
1 small onion, finely chopped
2 tbsp oil
salt

1 Cut the aubergines into large chunks, peel and cube the potatoes and leave the vegetables in a pan of cold water to prevent discoloration while you prepare the spices.

2 In a liquidizer, blend together the ginger, garlic, coriander leaves, powdered spices, tamarind juice and onion.

3 Heat the oil in a pan and add the blended spices. Stir and fry for 3–4 minutes, until the oil runs clear of the spices.

4 Drain the vegetables, add them to the pan and cook, tightly covered, over a low heat for 15–20 minutes, until tender. Add 1–2 tbsp water during the cooking if necessary and stir occasionally to prevent the vegetables from sticking.

5 Add salt to taste.

Spicy Aubergine
(*Baigan bharta*)

SERVES 2
450 g/1 lb aubergines
3 tbsp oil
1 large onion, finely chopped
3 tomatoes, chopped
1 tbsp coriander leaves, chopped
1–2 green chillies, chopped
½ tsp ground turmeric
½ tsp chilli powder
¾ tsp ground coriander
¾ tsp salt

1 Place the aubergines under a preheated grill for about 15 minutes, turning frequently until the skin turns black and the flesh soft. Peel off the skin and mash the flesh.

2 Heat the oil in a karai over medium heat and fry the onions until soft. Add the tomatoes, coriander leaves and green chillies and fry another 2–3 minutes.

3 Add the mashed aubergine, turmeric, chilli, coriander and salt and stir.

4 Fry for another 10–12 minutes and serve with Chappatis (see page 146).

Aubergine with Sour Cream
(*Malai baigan*)

SERVES 2

1 large aubergine, cut into 1 cm/½ in
   slices
½ tsp salt
½ tsp ground turmeric
pinch of sugar
8 tbsp oil
pinch of asafoetida
2 tbsp onion mixture (see page 22)
1 tsp ground cumin
1 tsp ground coriander
½ tsp chilli powder
big pinch of sugar
½ tsp salt
150 g/5 oz sour cream

1 Rub the aubergine slices with ½ tsp salt, ½ tsp turmeric and a pinch of sugar and set aside for 30 minutes.

2 Heat the oil in a large frying pan over medium high heat and fry the aubergine slices until brown. Drain on paper towels.

3 Lower the heat to medium and add the asafoetida to the remaining oil. Fry for 3–4 seconds and then add the onion mixture, cumin, coriander, chilli, sugar and salt and fry for 2 minutes.

4 Add the sour cream and mix with the spices. Add the fried aubergine slices. Cover and cook for 10 minutes. Serve with Chappatis (see page 146).

Opposite Spicy aubergine/
Baigan bharta

Below Aubergine with sour cream/
Malai baigan

Okra Curry
(Bhindi curry)

SERVES 2
225 g/8 oz okra
3 tbsp oil
grated flesh of ½ coconut
½ tsp chilli powder
½ tsp turmeric
½ tsp ground cumin
225 g/8 oz yoghurt
½ tsp mustard seeds
I red chilli, cut into pieces
leaves from I sprig of coriander,
    chopped
4–6 curry leaves
salt

1 Wash the okra and dry them on absorbent kitchen paper. Cut into 2.5 cm/2 in lengths.

2 Heat 1 tbsp oil and fry the okra for about 2 minutes, turning gently, until all the oil has been absorbed. Remove with a slotted spoon and set aside.

3 Blend the coconut with the chilli powder, turmeric and cumin in a liquidizer, adding 1 tbsp water to make a smooth paste. Mix this into the yoghurt.

4 Heat the remaining oil and when hot, add the mustard seeds and red chilli. Let them sizzle for a few seconds, until all the seeds have popped, then add the okra.

5 Turn the heat down and add the yoghurt mix. Cook gently for 2–3 minutes, stirring to prevent the yoghurt from separating, until hot through. Add the coriander and curry leaves, and salt to taste.

Masala Aubergine
(Tel baigan)

SERVES 2
I large aubergine, cut into large
    pieces
½ tsp salt
big pinch of turmeric
8 tbsp mustard oil
½ tsp kalonji
¾ tsp ground turmeric
½ tsp chilli powder
½ tsp salt
¼ tsp sugar
4 tbsp yoghurt
50 ml/2 fl oz water
2–3 green chillies
I tsp ground roasted cumin seeds
    (see page 23)

1 Rub the aubergine pieces with the ½ tsp salt and a big pinch of turmeric and set aside for 30 minutes.

2 Heat the oil in a karai over high heat and fry the aubergines until brown. Drain on paper towels.

3 Lower the heat to medium and add the kalonji. After 4–5 seconds add the turmeric, chilli powder, salt, sugar and yoghurt. Stir fry for 1 minute.

4 Add the water; when it starts to boil add the aubergines and green chillies and cook for 5 minutes.

5 Before removing from the heat sprinkle with the ground roasted cumin. Serve with rice.

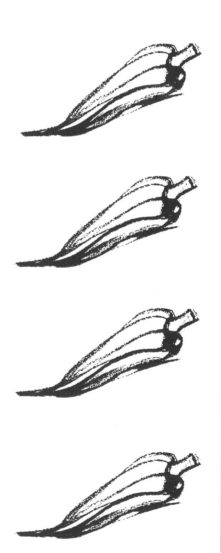

92

Mashed Aubergine
(Baigan bharta)

SERVES 2

1 aubergine
50–75 g/2–3 oz butter or ghee
1 onion, finely chopped
leaves from 1 sprig of coriander
1 clove garlic, chopped
15 g/½ oz fresh ginger, finely grated
½ tsp garam masala
1 green chilli, sliced
½ tsp turmeric
½ tsp cumin
½ tsp chilli powder
225 g/8 oz tomatoes, peeled and
    chopped
salt
1 tbsp lemon juice

1 Put the aubergine in a roasting tin and cook in the oven at 200°C/400°F/Gas 6 for 40 minutes or until the inside is cooked. Allow the aubergine to cool, then peel off the skin and immerse the vegetable in cold water.

2 Heat the butter or ghee in a pan and add the onion, half the coriander leaves, the garlic, ginger, garam masala, green chilli, turmeric, cumin and chilli powder. Stir and fry until the onion is golden.

3 Add the tomatoes, squashing well with the back of a wooden spoon to make a paste.

Above Mashed aubergine/
Baigan bharta

4 Meanwhile, drain the aubergine and mash with a fork.

5 When the butter runs out of the spice paste, add the aubergine and ½ tsp salt, stir thoroughly and cook for 3–4 minutes to heat through.

6 Sprinkle on the remaining coriander leaves and the lemon juice. Add more salt to taste if liked.

Okra Toran
(Bhindi toran)

SERVES 2
300 g/10 oz okra
3 tbsp oil
½ tsp mustard seeds
1 tsp polished split black lentils
   (urid dal)
1 small onion, chopped
15 g/½ oz fresh ginger, finely grated
2 green chillies, chopped
25–50 g/1–2 oz grated or desiccated
   coconut
4–6 curry leaves
salt

1 Wash the okra and dry on absorbent kitchen paper. Cut into 2 cm/¾ in lengths.

2 Fry the okra in 2 tbsp oil, turning frequently, until all the oil has been absorbed. This seals the okra and helps them keep their shape during cooking. Remove the okra from the pan with a slotted spoon and set aside.

3 Add the remaining oil to the pan and when hot, add the mustard seeds and dal. Let them sizzle for a few seconds until all the mustard seeds have popped and the dal is golden, then add the onion and fry until golden.

4 Add the ginger and green chilli and continue to fry for 3–4 minutes. Stir in the coconut and curry leaves. Add salt to taste.

Fried Okra with Onions
(Bhindi bhaji)

SERVES 2–3
450 g/1 lb okra
3 tbsp oil
2 large onions, finely chopped
1 tsp salt

1 Wash the okra and pat dry with absorbent kitchen paper.

2 Cut into 1 cm/½ in pieces.

3 Heat the oil in a karai over medium heat and fry the onions until soft.

4 Add the okra and salt, and, stirring gently, continue frying until the okra is cooked, about 10–12 minutes. Serve with rice and lentils or Paratha (see page 147).

Fried Spiced Okra
(*Bhindi masala*)

SERVES 2
225 g/8 oz okra
50 g/2 oz butter or ghee
I small onion, finely chopped
I clove garlic, finely chopped
I green chilli, chopped
15 g/½ oz fresh ginger, finely grated
leaves from I sprig of coriander
100 g/4 oz tomatoes, peeled and
  roughly chopped
½ tsp ground coriander
½ tsp turmeric
½ tsp chilli powder
I tsp garam masala
salt

1 Wash the okra and dry them on absorbent kitchen paper. Cut into 2.5 cm/1 in lengths. Heat half the butter or ghee in a pan, add the okra and fry gently. Keep turning them so that they are cooked on all sides, until most of the fat has been absorbed (about 2 minutes). Remove with a slotted spoon and set aside.

2 Add the remaining butter or ghee to the pan and when hot, add the onion, garlic, green chilli, ginger and coriander leaves. Stir and fry until the onion is golden.

3 Add the tomato, ground coriander, turmeric, chilli powder and garam masala and continue to cook, mashing the tomato under the back of a wooden spoon to make a paste.

4 When the butter runs clear of the spices, add the okra and cook on a low heat, stirring occasionally, for about 10 minutes. Add salt to taste.

Okra with Yoghurt
(*Dahi bhindi*)

SERVES 2–3
450 g/I lb okra
4 tbsp oil
½ tsp panch phoron
I cm/½ in ginger, grated
2 green chillies, cut lengthwise
big pinch of turmeric
½ tsp salt
150 ml/¼ pt yoghurt
8–10 curry leaves

1 Wash the okra and pat dry on kitchen towels. Cut into 2.5 cm/1 in pieces.

2 Heat the oil in a karai over medium high heat, add the panch phoron, ginger and chillies. Let them sizzle for a few seconds.

3 Add the okra and, stirring gently, fry for 5 minutes. Lower the heat to medium low.

4 Add the turmeric, salt and yoghurt and mix gently with the okra. Cover and cook for 10 minutes.

5 Add the curry leaves and cook a further 5 minutes. Serve with rice or Poori (see page 152).

Opposite Fried okra with onions/
Bhindi bhaji

Left Okra with yoghurt/Dahi bhindi

Fried Bitter Gourd
(*Karela masala*)

SERVES 2
225 g/8 oz bitter gourds
salt
4 tbsp oil
1 green chilli, sliced
15 g/½ oz fresh ginger, finely grated
6–8 curry leaves
2 tbsp lemon juice

1 Scrape the gourds and cut into 2 cm/¾ in slices. Sprinkle with 1 tsp salt and leave in a cool place for 10 minutes. Rinse carefully and dry on absorbent kitchen paper.

2 Heat the oil in a pan and add the gourds, green chilli, ginger and curry leaves. Fry for 10–15 minutes, stirring, until the gourd is cooked.

3 Sprinkle over the lemon juice and add salt to taste.

Right Fried bitter gourd/
Karela masala

Stuffed Okra
(*Sabu bhindi*)

SERVES 2
225 g/8 oz okra
½ tsp paprika
½ tsp chilli powder
1 tbsp mango powder (amchur)
½ tsp ground ginger
salt
4 tbsp oil

1 Wash the okra and dry on absorbent kitchen paper. Cut off the stalks and slice the okra in half lengthways.

2 Mix together the spices and salt.

3 Stuff the okra with the spice mix and leave them to stand in a cool place for at least 30 minutes.

4 Heat the oil and fry the okra for about 4 minutes, turning carefully, to cook on all sides.

Below Stuffed okra/Sabu bhindi

Stuffed Bitter Gourds
(*Sabu karela*)

SERVES 4
450 g/1 lb bitter gourds
1 tsp salt
1 tsp chilli powder
2 tbsp mango powder (amchur)
4 tbsp oil

1 Scrape the gourds and slit them lengthways from the tip, leaving the 2 halves joined at the stalk. Sprinkle salt both inside and out and leave the gourds in a cool place for 15 minutes.

2 Scrape away the seeds and squeeze the gourds to remove the moisture drawn from them by the salt.

3 Mix together the chilli powder, mango powder and remaining salt.

4 Sprinkle the insides of the gourds with oil and stuff the spice mixture well down inside them. Tie the gourds together with thread.

5 Heat the remaining oil over a low heat and fry the gourds, turning gently for 5–10 minutes, until cooked. Remove the thread.

6 Serve hot or cold.

Bitter Gourd with Onion Stuffing
(*Piyaz karela*)

SERVES 2
225 g/8 oz bitter gourds
salt
1 onion, finely chopped
1 tsp chilli powder
15 g/½ oz fresh ginger, finely grated
2 tbsp lemon juice
4 tbsp oil

1 Scrape the gourds and slit them lengthways from the tip, leaving the 2 halves joined at the stalk. Sprinkle salt both inside and out and leave the gourds in a cool place for 15 minutes.

2 Scrape away the seeds and squeeze the gourds to remove the moisture drawn from them by the salt.

3 In a liquidizer, blend together the onion, chilli, ½ tsp salt and the ginger, then mix in the lemon juice

4 Stuff the gourds with the onion mixture and tie them together with thread. Leave to stand for 5–10 minutes.

5 Heat the oil in a pan, add the gourds and fry over a low heat, turning gently, for 5–10 minutes, until done.

Right Stuffed bitter gourds/
Sabu karela

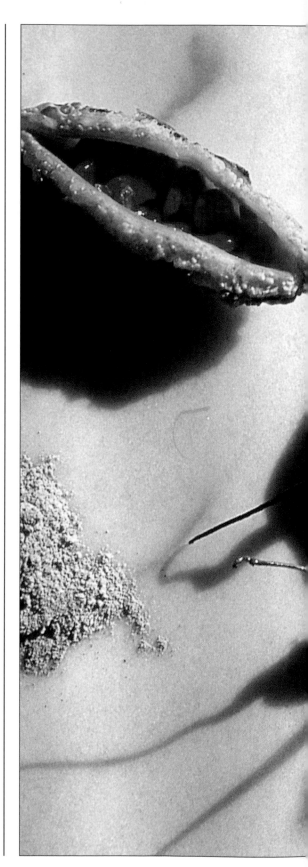

Meat

· ·

Goat is the meat most often eaten in India, and lamb is the best substitute. Shoulder or neck are the best cuts to buy as they have more connective tissue. This means that they can be cooked for a fairly long time and end up succulent and tender.

All recipes in this section are intended for boned meat, but the bones can be left in. If you wish to do this, allow for the weight of the bones, which will be about half the total weight of the meat.

Beef and pork may also be used, although beef is not often eaten in India. For the Hindus, the cow is a sacred animal, and the Muslims are forbidden pork.

Meat Kebabs
(*Seekh kebabs*)

SERVES 4
15 g/½ oz fresh ginger, finely grated
1 green chilli, chopped
salt
½ tsp garam masala
450 g/1 lb lean minced meat
1 onion, finely chopped
½ tsp chilli powder
½ tsp ground pepper
½ tsp ground cumin
leaves from 1 sprig of coriander
1 egg, beaten
6 tbsp oil

1 Grind, pound or blend in a liquidizer the ginger, green chilli, ½ tsp salt and the garam masala with 1–2 tbsp water to make a paste.

2 In a bowl, mix the spice paste with the meat and onion, sprinkle on the chilli powder, pepper, cumin and coriander leaves, add the egg and 1–2 tsp oil and combine well.

3 Roll the mixture into small sausages and thread on skewers.

4 Grill the kebabs for 20 minutes, basting with a little oil, and turning frequently until cooked through.

5 Remove the kebabs from the skewers and fry in the remaining oil for about 10 minutes, turning gently.

Photograph on page 100.

Above Meat and vegetable curry/
Sabzi gosht

Meat and Vegetable Curry
(*Sabzi gosht*)

SERVES 4
75 g/3 oz butter or ghee
1 small onion, finely chopped
15 g/½ oz fresh ginger, grated
2 cloves garlic, chopped
½ tsp turmeric
½ tsp chilli powder
½ tsp ground coriander
½ tsp garam masala
½ tsp ground cumin
1 green chilli, chopped
4–6 curry leaves
450 g/1 lb meat, trimmed and cubed
175 g/6 oz tomatoes, peeled and
    chopped
100 g/4 oz okra, trimmed and cut
    into 2 or 3 pieces
100 g/4 oz carrots, peeled and diced
225 g/8 oz potatoes, peeled and
    cubed
175 g/6 oz aubergine, peeled and
    cubed
50 g/2 oz fresh peas
salt

1 Heat the butter or ghee in a pan, add the onion and fry until golden.

2 Add the ginger, garlic, turmeric, chilli powder, coriander, garam masala, cumin, green chilli and curry leaves, stir and fry for a further 5 minutes.

3 Add the meat and fry for 5 minutes, then add the tomato, okra, carrot, potato, aubergine and peas, pour on 900 ml/1½ pt water, add ½ tsp salt and cook over a low heat for 1 hour, until the vegetables and meat are tender and the sauce is thick.

4 Add extra salt to taste.

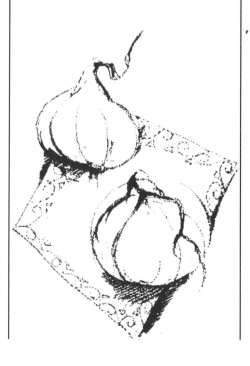

Pork Vindaloo
(Soor vindaloo)

SERVES 4
6 cloves garlic
25 g/1 oz fresh ginger
4 red chillies, seeded
1 tsp mustard seeds
½ tsp fenugreek seeds
½ tsp turmeric
½ tsp ground cumin
4 tbsp white wine vinegar
2–3 tbsp oil
2 onions, finely chopped
225 g/8 oz tomatoes, peeled and
    chopped
1–1.4 kg/2 lb 3 oz–3 lb shoulder of
    pork, trimmed and cubed
salt
600 ml/1 pt boiling water

4–6 curry leaves
6 cloves
2.5 cm/1 in cinnamon stick
1 tsp sugar

1 Chop 4 cloves garlic with half the ginger, then grind, pound or blend in a liquidizer with the chillies, mustard seeds, fenugreek seeds, turmeric and half the vinegar.

2 Heat the oil, add the onion and fry until golden.

3 Add the spice paste, stir and fry gently for 15 minutes.

4 Add the tomato and continue to cook, mashing it under the back of a wooden spoon to make a paste.

5 When the oil has run clear of the spices, add the pork and fry for 5 minutes, turning the pieces in the spice mixture.

6 Add ½ tsp salt and pour on the boiling water. Simmer, covered, for 40 minutes, until the pork is tender.

7 Slice the remaining garlic and ginger and add with the curry leaves, cloves and cinnamon stick. Cook for a further 5 minutes.

8 Add the sugar and remaining vinegar. Add salt to taste.

Below Pork vindaloo/Soor vindaloo

Meat Curry with Nuts and Coconut Milk
(*Narial gosht*)

SERVES 4

flesh of 1 coconut, grated

50 g/2 oz cashew nuts

2 cloves garlic, chopped

½ tsp chilli powder

15 g/½ oz fresh ginger, grated

½ tsp ground coriander

½ tsp turmeric

leaves from 1 sprig of coriander

½ tsp garam masala

½ tsp ground pepper

100 g/4 oz butter or ghee

1 small onion, chopped

1 kg/2lb 3oz meat, trimmed and
  cubed

¼ tsp saffron

25 g/1 oz sultanas

50 g/2 oz almonds

salt

4–6 curry leaves

1 Blend the coconut in a liquidizer with 1 tbsp boiling water. Transfer to a sheet of muslin and squeeze out the milk into a bowl. Return the coconut to the liquidizer and repeat the process.

2 Grind, pound or blend in a liquidizer the cashew nuts, garlic, chilli powder, ginger, ground coriander, turmeric, coriander leaves, garam masala and pepper.

3 Heat the butter or ghee in a pan, add the onion and fry until golden, then add the blended spices and fry for a further 5 minutes.

4 Add the meat, stir and fry for 5 minutes, then pour on the coconut milk, add the saffron, sultanas, almonds and ½ tsp salt and cook, covered, over a low heat for about 1 hour, until the meat is tender and the sauce has thickened.

5 Sprinkle on the curry leaves.

Below Meat curry with nuts and coconut milk/Narial gosht

Above Meatball and cauliflower
curry/Phul gobi kofta

Meatball and Cauliflower Curry
(Phul gobi kofta)

SERVES 4

Meat and Cauliflower

1 egg, beaten
450 g/1 lb lean minced meat
15 g/½ oz fresh ginger, grated
2 cloves garlic, chopped
½ tsp garam masala
½ tsp ground cumin
leaves from 1 sprig of coriander
salt
1 small cauliflower, cut into florets,
    tough stalks discarded

Sauce

75 g/3 oz butter or ghee
1 small onion, finely chopped
cardamom seeds from 2 pods,
    crushed
2 cloves
2.5 cm/1 in cinnamon stick
15 g/½ oz fresh ginger, grated

2 cloves garlic, crushed
½ tsp turmeric
1 tsp chilli powder
½ tsp ground cumin
½ tsp ground coriander
225 g/8 oz tomatoes, peeled and
    chopped or 2 tbsp tomato purée
150 ml/¼ pt yoghurt
salt
leaves from 1 sprig of coriander

1 Mix the egg with the minced
meat.

2 Grind, pound or blend in a
liquidizer the ginger, garlic, garam
masala, cumin, coriander leaves
and ½ tsp salt.

3 Mix the spice paste with the
meat, form it into small balls and
set aside.

4 To make the sauce, heat the

butter or ghee in a pan, add the
onion and fry until golden.

5 Add the cardamom seeds, cloves,
cinnamon, ginger, garlic, turmeric,
chilli powder, cumin and coriander
and fry for 3 or 4 minutes, stirring.

6 Add the tomato or tomato purée
and cook, stirring, until the fat runs
clear of the spices.

7 Stir in the yoghurt with a pinch
of salt and 1–2 tbsp water and bring
gently to the boil.

8 Carefully slide in the meat balls
and cauliflower florets and cook for
about 20 minutes on a low heat,
stirring occasionally and taking
care not to break the meat balls.

9 Sprinkle on the coriander leaves
and add salt to taste.

Above Sweet and sour meat curry/
Chuteraney

Sweet and Sour Meat Curry
(Chuteraney)

SERVES 4
2 tbsp oil
50 g/2 oz butter or ghee
2 onions, finely chopped
1 green chilli, chopped
15 g/½ oz fresh ginger, finely grated
2 cloves garlic, crushed
225 g/8 oz tomatoes, peeled and
   chopped
leaves from 2 sprigs of coriander
½ tsp garam masala
½ tsp turmeric
1 tsp chilli powder
1 kg/2lb 3 oz meat, trimmed and
   cubed
600 ml/1 pt boiling water
225 g/8 oz potatoes, peeled and
   chopped
½ tsp ground pepper
1 tbsp sugar
150 ml/¼ pt yoghurt

2 tbsp lemon juice
salt

1 Heat the oil and butter or ghee in a pan, add the onion, green chilli, ginger and garlic and fry until the onion turns golden.

2 Add the tomato, half the coriander leaves, the garam masala, turmeric and chilli powder and cook, stirring and squashing the tomato under the back of a wooden spoon until it makes a paste and the fat has run clear of the spices.

3 Add the meat and boiling water and cook over a low heat for about 1 hour, until tender.

4 Add the potato and cook for a further 10–15 minutes until tender but not soft.

5 Mix the remaining coriander leaves, the pepper and sugar with the yoghurt, add to the curry and cook for 2–3 minutes, stirring, to heat through.

6 Sprinkle on the lemon juice and add salt to taste.

Opposite Meat curry with roasted
spices/Masala gosht

Meat Curry with Roasted Spices
(*Masala gosht*)

SERVES 4

3 tbsp oil
2 tbsp coriander seeds
2 red chillies, cut into pieces
2.5 cm/1 in cinnamon stick
3 cloves
50 g/2 oz grated coconut
450 g/1 lb meat, trimmed and cubed
½ tsp turmeric
salt
2 green chillies, sliced
15 g/½ oz fresh ginger, grated
1 small onion, chopped

225 g/8 oz potatoes, peeled and diced
225 g/8 oz tomatoes, peeled and chopped
900 ml/1 ½ pt boiling water
6 curry leaves

1 Heat half the oil in a pan and fry the coriander seeds, red chilli, cinnamon, cloves and coconut for about 5 minutes, then transfer to a grinder or a mortar and reduce to a smooth paste.

2 Put the meat in a bowl with the turmeric, ½ tsp salt, green chilli, ginger and half the onion, add the spice paste and mix well. Leave to marinate for 15 minutes.

3 Heat the remaining oil in a large saucepan and fry the remaining onion until golden.

4 Add the marinated meat, the potato and tomato, pour on the boiling water, cover and cook on a low heat for about 1 hour, until the meat is tender and the sauce is thick.

5 Add extra salt to taste and sprinkle on the curry leaves.

Plain Meat Curry
(*Gosht curry*)

SERVES 4

1 kg/2 lb 3 oz meat, trimmed and
   cubed
600 ml/1 pt water
1 tbsp lemon juice
salt
2 tbsp ground coriander
2 tsp chilli powder
½ tsp ground pepper
1 tsp ground cumin
½ tsp turmeric
50 g/2 oz butter or ghee
1 tbsp oil
1 small onion, finely chopped
25 g/1 oz fresh ginger, chopped
2 cloves garlic, chopped
1 tsp garam masala
4–6 curry leaves

1 Wash the meat thoroughly in hot water. Drain and cook, covered, in the measured amount of water with the lemon juice and a pinch of salt for about an hour or until the meat is tender and most of the liquid has evaporated.

2 Mix the coriander, chilli, pepper, cumin and turmeric with 2 tbsp water to make a smooth paste.

3 Heat the butter or ghee in a pan with the oil, add the onion, ginger and garlic and fry until the onion is golden.

4 Add the spice paste and continue to fry for 10 minutes. Add the paste to the cooked meat with ½ tsp salt and cook, covered, on a low heat for 10–15 minutes, until the sauce is thick.

5 Sprinkle on the garam masala and the curry leaves and add extra salt to taste.

Meat and Tomato Curry
(*Tamatar gosht*)

SERVES 4

50 g/2 oz butter or ghee
1 small onion, finely chopped
15 g/½ oz fresh ginger, finely grated
3 cloves garlic, finely chopped
225 g/8 oz tomatoes, peeled and
   chopped
½ tsp turmeric
2 tsp chilli powder
1 tbsp ground coriander
½ tsp ground cumin
salt
1 tsp garam masala
600 ml/1 pt boiling water
1 kg/2 lb 3 oz meat, trimmed and
   cubed
225 g/8 oz potatoes, peeled and
   diced
leaves from 1 sprig of coriander

1 Heat the butter or ghee in a large saucepan, add the onion, ginger and garlic and fry until the onion is golden.

2 Add the tomato, turmeric, chilli powder, ground coriander, cumin, ½ tsp salt and garam masala. Stir and continue to fry until the fat runs clear of the spices, then add the boiling water and mix well.

3 Add the meat and cook, covered, over a low heat for about 1 hour, until tender and the sauce is thick.

4 Add the potato and a little extra water, if necessary, and cook for a further 10–15 minutes until tender but not soft.

5 Sprinkle on the coriander leaves and extra salt to taste.

Below Meat and tomato curry/
Tamatar gosht

Fried Spiced Meat Keema
(Keema masala)

SERVES 4
100 g/4 oz butter or ghee
1 onion, finely chopped
2 cloves garlic, finely chopped
15 g/½ oz fresh ginger, finely grated
leaves from 1 sprig of coriander
175 g/6 oz tomatoes, peeled and
    chopped
cardamom seeds from 2 pods,
    crushed
2.5 cm/1 in cinnamon stick
3 cloves
1 bay leaf
½ tsp ground coriander
½ tsp turmeric
½ tsp ground cumin
½ tsp chilli powder

salt
450 g/1 lb lean minced meat
225 g/8 oz potatoes, peeled and
    diced
300 ml/½ pt boiling water

1 Heat the butter or ghee in a pan, add the onion and fry until golden.

2 Add the garlic, ginger, half the coriander leaves, the tomato, cardomom, cinnamon, cloves and bay leaf and fry for 3–4 minutes, stirring.

3 Add the coriander, turmeric, cumin, chilli powder and ½ tsp salt and stir to make a thick paste.

4 Add the meat and potato and fry for about 15 minutes, stirring occa-sionally, then pour on the boiling water, cover and cook on a low heat for a further 15 minutes, until the meat and potato are cooked and the sauce is thick.

5 Add salt to taste and sprinkle on the remaining coriander leaves.

Above Fried spiced meat keema/
Keema masala

109

Meat Curry in a Thick Sauce
(*Gosht dupiaza*)

SERVES 4

I small onion, finely chopped
2 tbsp oil
I tbsp plain flour
I kg/2 lb 3 oz meat, trimmed and
   cubed
I tbsp lemon juice
½ tsp ground pepper
salt
900 ml/I ½ pt water
50 g/2 oz butter or ghee
225 g/8 oz tomatoes, chopped
I green chilli, sliced
leaves from I sprig of coriander
½ tsp garam masala

1 Fry the onion in the oil until golden. Add the flour and continue to fry, stirring, until the flour is coloured and has formed a paste.

2 Add the meat, lemon juice, pepper and ½ tsp salt, stir and pour on the water. Bring to the boil and simmer, covered, for about 1 hour, stirring occasionally, until the meat is tender and the sauce is thick.

3 Heat the butter or ghee in a pan, add the tomato and green chilli and fry gently, stirring, for 3–4 minutes, then add to the meat.

4 Sprinkle on the coriander leaves and garam masala.

Below Meat curry in thick sauce/
Gosht dupiaza

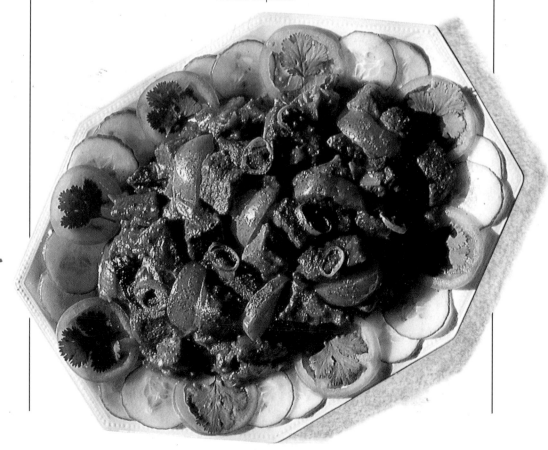

Meat Curry with Yoghurt
(Dahi gosht)

SERVES 4

4–6 tbsp oil
2 onions, roughly chopped
25 g/1 oz fresh ginger, chopped
2 cloves garlic, chopped
1 green chilli, chopped
cardamom seeds from 2 pods
2.5 cm/1 in cinnamon stick
3 cloves
½ tsp fennel seeds
1 tbsp ground coriander
1 tsp ground cumin
leaves from 2 sprigs coriander
½ tsp turmeric
1 tsp chilli powder
150 ml/¼ pt yoghurt
1 kg/2 lb 3 oz meat, trimmed and
    cubed
600 ml/1 pt boiling water
4–6 curry leaves

1 Heat half the oil in a pan, add half the onion, the ginger, garlic, green chilli, cardamom seeds, cinnamon, cloves, fennel seeds, ground coriander, cumin, half the coriander leaves, the turmeric and chilli and fry gently, stirring, for 10 minutes.

2 Take the pan off the heat and stir in the yoghurt. Mix well and set aside.

3 Chop the remaining onion finely and fry in the remaining oil until golden. Add the cubed meat and fry for about 15 minutes, stirring occasionally.

4 Stir in the spiced yoghurt and cook gently for 8–10 minutes, stirring.

5 Pour on the boiling water, turn down the heat and cook, covered, for about 1 hour or until the meat is tender. Cook uncovered if a thicker sauce is required and stir frequently.

6 Sprinkle on the curry leaves and remaining coriander leaves and add salt to taste.

Below Meat curry with yoghurt/
Dahi gosht

Lamb with Cardamom
(Elaichi gosht)

SERVES 4–6
30 black peppercorns
25 cardamom pods, skinned
5 medium tomatoes
2.5 cm/1 in ginger, cut into small
  pieces
120 ml/4 fl oz oil
2 large onions, finely chopped
1 kg/2 lb lamb, cut into 2.5 cm/1 in
  cubes
2 tsp paprika
1½ tsp salt
250 ml/8 fl oz water
3 tbsp coriander leaves, chopped

1 Grind the peppercorns and cardamom seeds finely.

2 In a liquidizer or processor, blend the tomatoes and ginger.

3 Heat the oil in a saucepan and fry the onions until golden. Add the meat and the ground spices. Stir constantly and fry for 5 minutes.

4 Add the blended mixture, paprika and salt, mix with the meat and fry for a further 2–3 minutes.

5 Add the water, bring it to a boil, cover, lower the heat to very low and cook for about 1 hour until tender. Garnish with coriander leaves and serve with rice.

Meat cooked with Wheat Grains
(Haleem)

SERVES 4–6
450 g/1 lb whole wheat grains
5 cardamom pods
2.5 cm/1 in cinnamon stick
6 cloves
2.5 cm/1 in ginger
4 cloves garlic
175 g/6 oz ghee (see page 21)
4 medium onions, finely sliced
700 g/1½ lb boneless lamb, cut into
  2.5 cm/1 in cubes
1 tsp ground turmeric
2 tsp chilli powder
1 tbsp ground poppy seeds
3 tbsp desiccated coconut

Above Lamb with cardamom/
Elaichi gosht

2 tbsp chopped coriander leaves
1 tbsp chopped mint leaves
2 tsp salt
175 ml/6 fl oz yoghurt
juice of 2 limes

1 Soak the wheat in plenty of water overnight. Drain. Place the wheat and some water in a large saucepan and bring to a boil. Cook until it is tender and mushy.

2 Grind the cardamom, cinnamon and cloves to a fine powder.

3 Grind the ginger and garlic to a fine paste.

4 In a large saucepan, heat the ghee and fry the onions until golden. Remove one third of the fried onions and put aside.

5 Add the ginger and garlic paste, the lamb, turmeric, chilli powder, poppy seeds, coconut, coriander and mint leaves, the salt and half the ground spices and stir fry for 5–6 minutes.

6 Add the yoghurt and mix thoroughly. Lower the heat. Cover and cook for about 30 minutes.

7 Add the remaining ground spices and continue to cook for about another 30 minutes until the meat is tender. Remove from the heat.

8 Add the boiled wheat and beat with the back of a wooden spoon until the meat disintegrates.

9 Add the lime juice and stir well. Bring to a boil again and boil for 5 minutes.

10 Serve garnished with the remaining fried onions.

An alternative method is to lift the cooked meat out of the gravy and blend it with the wheat in a food processor, until coarsely ground. Then put it back into the gravy and continue from point 9 above.

Lamb Chop Kebabs
(*Bara kabab*)

SERVES 4
700 g/1 ½ lb lamb chops
475 ml/16 fl oz yoghurt
1 ½ tsp salt
2.5 cm/1 in ginger, grated
8 cloves garlic, crushed
¾ tsp garam masala powder
1 tbsp poppy seeds, ground
2–3 green chillies, ground
2 tbsp oil

1 Remove excess fat from the chops. Wash and pat dry.

2 Lightly beat the yoghurt and mix in all the ingredients.

3 Add the lamb chops and marin- ate for at least 6 hours. It is best to marinate for 24 hours – if you are going to marinate for this long, cover and refrigerate the meat but make sure it is returned to room temperature before it is grilled.

4 Preheat the grill.

5 Take the chops out of the marinade and place on a baking sheet. Grill for 8–10 minutes on each side.

Below Lamb chop kebabs/
Bara kabab

Chicken

. . . .

In India chicken used to be a special treat and many spectacular and elegant dishes were devised to make the most of it. Today, however, it makes quite a regular appearance at the tables of meat-eating families.

You can use chicken joints for most of the recipes in this section, or buy a whole bird and cut it up into smaller pieces yourself. Indians mostly skin chicken before cooking it to allow the aromatics to permeate the meat.

Chicken Curry with Yoghurt
(*Murghi dahi*)

SERVES 4

4 tbsp oil
2 onions, finely chopped
2 cloves garlic, finely chopped
15 g/½ oz fresh ginger, finely grated
cardamom seeds from 2 pods
2.5 cm/1 in cinnamon stick
2 cloves
½ tsp fennel seeds
1 tsp paprika
2 tsp ground coriander
½ tsp ground cumin
½ tsp chilli powder
½ tsp turmeric
150 ml/¼ pt yoghurt

1.4 kg/3 lb chicken, skinned and jointed
225 g/8 oz potatoes, peeled and diced
225 g/8 oz tomatoes, peeled and chopped
salt
900 ml/1½ pt boiling water
leaves from 2 sprigs of coriander

1 Heat 3 tbsp oil in a pan, add the onion, garlic, ginger, cardamom seeds, cinnamon, cloves and fennel seeds and fry until the onion is golden.

2 Add the paprika, coriander, cumin, chilli powder and turmeric and continue to fry until the oil runs free from the spice mixture.

3 Drain off the oil, stir in the yoghurt and blend in a liquidizer until smooth.

4 Fry the remaining onion in the remaining oil until golden, add the chicken and continue to fry for 5 minutes.

5 Add the blended spice mixture, the potato, tomato, ½ tsp salt and boiling water and cook on a low heat for about 1 hour, until the meat and vegetables are done.

6 Add extra salt to taste and sprinkle over the coriander leaves.

Below Chicken curry with yoghurt/Murghi dahi

Spiced Chicken
(Murghi masala)

SERVES 4

3 tbsp coriander seeds
2 red chillies, cut into 3 or 4 pieces
2.5 cm/1 in cinnamon stick
2 cloves
50 g/2 oz grated coconut
½ tsp turmeric
2 onions, finely chopped
15 g/½ oz fresh ginger, finely grated
4–6 curry leaves
1 kg/2 lb 3 oz chicken joints, skinned
3 tbsp oil
2 green chillies, seeded and cut into
    3 or 4 pieces
2 bay leaves
900 ml/1½ pt water
100 g/4 oz tomatoes, peeled and
    chopped
salt

1 Heat a pan without any fat or oil until very hot, then add the coriander seeds, red chilli, cinnamon stick and cloves, and roast them for 5–6 minutes, shaking the pan to prevent them from burning. Grind or pound the roasted spices into a fine powder.

2 Blend the spices and coconut together in a liquidizer.

3 Stir in the turmeric, three-quarters of the onion, the ginger and half the curry leaves.

4 Smother the chicken with the spice mixture and leave to marinate for 10–15 minutes.

5 Heat the oil in a pan, add the remaining onion, green chilli and bay leaves. Fry until the onion is golden.

6 Add the water to the tomato and chicken pieces and cook gently, covered, for an hour, until the chicken is tender and the sauce is thick.

7 Add salt to taste.

Chicken and Tomato Curry
(Tamatar aur murghi)

SERVES 4

150 g/5 oz butter or ghee
2 onions, chopped
3 cloves garlic, crushed
15 g/½ oz fresh ginger, finely grated
1 green chilli, chopped
cardamom seeds from 2 pods,
    crushed
3 cloves
2.5 cm/1 in cinnamon stick
1 bay leaf
225 g/8 oz tomatoes, peeled and
    chopped
½ tsp turmeric
½ tsp chilli powder
½ tsp paprika
1 tbsp ground coriander
½ tsp fennel seeds
1 chicken, about 1.4 kg/3 lb, skinned
    and jointed
900 ml/1½ pt boiling water
225 g/8 oz potatoes, peeled and
    diced
¼ tsp ground pepper
¼ tsp saffron
salt
leaves from 2 sprigs of coriander

Above Chicken and tomato curry/
Tamatar aur murghi

1 Heat the butter or ghee in a pan, add the onion, garlic, ginger, green chilli, cardamom seeds, cloves, cinnamon and bay leaf and fry until the onion is golden.

2 Add the tomato and continue to cook, squashing it under the back of a wooden spoon to make a paste.

3 Add the turmeric, chilli powder, paprika, ground coriander and fennel seeds and fry until the fat runs clear of the spices.

4 Add the chicken pieces and fry for 5 minutes, then pour on the boiling water, add the potato and cook over a low heat, covered, for 1 hour, until the chicken and potato are done and the sauce has thickened.

5 Sprinkle on the pepper, saffron, salt and coriander leaves.

Chicken Biriyani
(*Murghi biriyani*)

SERVES 4–6
Chicken
1 tbsp biriyani masala
1 green chilli
15 g/½ oz fresh ginger, finely grated
2 cloves garlic, chopped
leaves from 2 sprigs coriander
1 tbsp chopped mint leaves
50 g/2 oz cashew nuts
6 tbsp oil
1.4 kg/3 lb chicken
50 g/2 oz butter or ghee
1 small onion, chopped
225 g/8 oz tomatoes, peeled and
    chopped
salt
600 ml/1 pt boiling water
Rice
100 g/4 oz butter or ghee
2 bay leaves
1 small onion, chopped
225 g/8 oz basmati rice, washed,
    soaked in water for 20 minutes
    and drained
600 ml/1 pt boiling water
10 cashew nuts
50 g/2 oz sultanas

1 Pound, grind or blend in a liquidizer the biriyani masala, green
chilli, ginger, garlic, coriander
leaves, mint and cashews, adding
about 2 tbsp water to make a paste.

2 Skin the chicken and cut into 8
pieces. Wash in hot water and dry
on absorbent kitchen paper.

3 Heat 4 tbsp oil in a pan, add the
chicken and fry for about 10 minutes,
turning once. Remove the chicken
with a slotted spoon and set aside.

4 Add the remaining oil and the
butter or ghee to the pan and when
hot, add the onion and fry until
golden.

5 Add the spice mixture and cook,
stirring, until the fat runs clear of
the spices.

6 Add the tomato, mashing it with
the back of a wooden spoon to
make a paste.

7 Add the chicken pieces and salt
and pour on the boiling water.
Cook for about 1 hour, until the
chicken is tender and the sauce has
thickened.

8 Meanwhile, for the rice, heat
three-quarters of the butter or ghee
in a heavy-based saucepan, add the
bay leaves and onion and fry until
the onion is golden.

9 Pour on the rice and stir well
over a low heat for about 10 minutes,
until the rice is translucent.

10 Add the boiling water, bring
back to the boil and cook on a low
heat, covered, for 8–10 minutes.
Drain off the water.

11 Mix the rice, chicken and sauce
together in an ovenproof casserole,
cover with a lid or foil and cook in
the oven at 150°C/300°F/Gas 2 for
10–15 minutes, until the rice is
completely cooked. This dish should
be moist but not too wet.

12 Fry the cashews and sultanas
briefly in the remaining butter or
ghee and sprinkle on top of the
curry.

Chicken Kebabs
(*Murghi kebabs*)

SERVES 2
2 tbsp soya sauce
2 tbsp oil
1 tsp ground black pepper
450 g/1 lb boned chicken, skinned
    and cubed

1 Mix the soya sauce, oil and
pepper with 1 tbsp water, pour over
the chicken, turn to coat and leave
to marinate for at least an hour.

2 Thread the chicken cubes on to
skewers and grill slowly for 25–30
minutes, turning and basting occasionally with the marinade, until
cooked through.

Photograph on page 114.

Opposite Chicken biriyani/
Murghi biriyani

Chicken with Spices
(*Murghi masala*)

SERVES 4
2–3 tbsp oil
2 cloves garlic, chopped
15 g/½ oz fresh ginger, finely grated
leaves from 1 sprig of coriander
½ tsp garam masala
1 tsp ground coriander
1 tsp ground cumin
4 cashew nuts
1 tbsp paprika
1 tsp chilli powder
1 tbsp lemon juice
1–2 tsp salt
150 ml/¼ pt yoghurt
8 chicken legs

1 In a liquidizer, blend all the ingredients except the chicken and yoghurt to a thick paste, then stir in the yoghurt and mix thoroughly.

2 Wash the chicken pieces, dry on absorbent kitchen paper and prick all over with a sharp pointed knife.

3 Smother the chicken in the spice paste and marinate for 3 hours.

4 Lay the chicken pieces on a rack across a roasting tin and cook in the oven at 200°C/400°F/Gas 6 for 45 minutes until the chicken is tender.

5 Sprinkle on extra salt to taste.

Above Chicken with spices/ Murghi masala

Above Chicken with honey/
Murghi madh

Chicken with Honey
(*Murghi madh*)

SERVES 4

15 g/½ oz fresh ginger, finely grated
2 cloves garlic, crushed
2 tbsp lemon juice
4 tbsp runny honey
1 tbsp paprika
1 tsp chilli powder
1 tbsp cornflour
½ tsp salt
8 chicken legs
1 tbsp lemon juice
leaves from 1–2 sprigs coriander

1 Put the ginger and the next 7 ingredients in a mortar or a liquidizer and pound or blend well to make a smooth paste.

2 Wash the chicken pieces, dry them on absorbent kitchen paper and prick them all over with a sharp, pointed knife.

3 Rub the spice paste all over the chicken and leave for at least 20 minutes to marinate.

4 Lay the chicken pieces on a rack across a roasting tin and cook in the oven at 200°C/400°F/Gas 6 for 45 minutes until the meat is cooked through.

5 Sprinkle over the lemon juice and garnish with coriander leaves.

Whole Roast Chicken
(*Murghi masala*)

Above Whole roast chicken/
Murghi masala

SERVES 4

1 chicken, about 1.4 kg/3 lb, skinned
½ tsp ground black pepper
salt
50 g/2 oz ground almonds
25 g/1 oz fresh ginger, finely grated
2 cloves garlic, chopped
leaves from 2 sprigs of coriander
1 onion, finely chopped
1 tsp garam masala
1 tsp paprika
1 tsp chilli powder
1 tsp ground coriander
¼ tsp saffron
1 tsp ground cumin
150 ml/¼ pt yoghurt
1 tbsp lemon juice

1 Skin and wash the chicken and dry with absorbent kitchen paper. Prick all over with a sharp pointed knife, rub in the black pepper and ½ tsp salt and leave to absorb the flavours for about 30 minutes.

2 Pound, grind or blend in a liquidizer the almond, ginger, garlic, coriander leaves, onion, garam masala, paprika, chilli powder, ground coriander, saffron and cumin, then mix well with the yoghurt.

3 Smother the chicken in the spiced yoghurt and marinate for at least 4 hours.

4 Put the chicken in a roasting tin and cook in the oven at 200°C/400°F/Gas 6, basting occasionally, for up to 2 hours until tender and the juices run clear when the bird is pierced with a skewer.

5 Sprinkle with lemon juice and salt to taste.

Chicken, Tandoori Style
(*Murghi tandoori*)

SERVES 4

8 chicken legs
1–2 tbsp lemon juice
salt
15 g/½ oz fresh ginger, finely grated
3 cloves garlic, chopped
1 tsp ground coriander
½ tsp ground cumin
1 tsp chilli powder
2 tbsp paprika
red food colouring (optional)
1 tsp garam masala
½ tsp ground black pepper
150 ml/¼ pt yoghurt
1 lemon, sliced
1 small onion, sliced

1 Skin the chicken legs, wash thoroughly and dry on absorbent kitchen paper. Slash them with a sharp pointed knife.

2 Rub in the lemon juice and sprinkle with salt.

3 Blend the ginger and garlic in a liquidizer with 1 tbsp water, then mix with the coriander, cumin, chilli powder, paprika, red food colouring, garam masala and pepper and stir into the yoghurt.

4 Smother the chicken legs in the spiced yoghurt and leave, covered, in the fridge to marinate overnight.

5 Lay the chicken legs on a rack across a roasting tin and cook in the oven at 200°C/400°F/Gas 6 for about 45 minutes, until tender.

6 Sprinkle with extra salt to taste and garnish with lemon and onion slices.

Below Chicken, tandoori style/ Murghi tandoori

123

Fish and Shellfish

· ·

There are said to be over 2000 varieties of fish and shellfish available in India, and it forms an important part of the diet, especially for non-meat eaters. The cold-water fish that swim in the seas around Europe and America are not natives to the warm waters of the Indian Ocean, but they are equally suited to Indian cooking. Best varieties are the firm-fleshed white fish such as cod, haddock or halibut.

Baked Fish stuffed with Mushrooms
(*Kumban machi*)

SERVES 4

2 tbsp oil

1 onion, sliced and separated into rings

15 g/½ oz fresh ginger, finely grated

1 tsp chopped mint leaves, fresh or bottled

225 g/8 oz tomatoes, peeled and chopped

½ tsp chilli powder

salt

225 g/8 oz mushrooms, peeled and sliced

450–700 g/1 – 1½ lb whole fish, such as cod, cleaned

2 tbsp lemon juice

1 Heat the oil in a pan, add the onion, ginger and mint and fry until the onion is golden.

2 Add the tomato, chilli powder and ½ tsp salt and cook, mashing the tomato into a thick paste with the back of a wooden spoon.

3 Add the mushroom and continue to cook for 6–7 minutes.

4 Use this mixture to stuff the fish. Lay it in a greased ovenproof dish, sprinkle with the remaining oil and the lemon juice, cover with foil and bake at 175°C/350°F/Gas 4 for 30–35 minutes, until tender.

5 Remove the skin and serve.

Below Baked fish with mushrooms/ Kumban machi

Fried Spiced Fish
(Machi masala)

SERVES 2

I onion, finely chopped
15 g/½ oz fresh ginger, finely grated
6 curry leaves
salt
¼ tsp turmeric
I tsp chilli powder
4 tbsp oil
450 g/I lb white fish, boned, skinned
   and cubed

1 Pound, grind or blend in a liquidizer the onion, ginger, curry leaves, ½ tsp salt, the turmeric and chilli powder to make a thick paste.

2 Spread the paste over the fish and leave to marinate for about 2 hours.

3 Heat the oil in a large pan that the fish will fit into in one layer, add the fish and fry for about 10 minutes, until tender.

4 Add extra salt to taste.

Sardines in a Thick Spicy Sauce
(Machli curry)

SERVES 4

3 tbsp oil
2 tbsp coriander seeds
3 red chillies, cut into pieces
50–75 g/2–3 oz grated coconut
I–2 tbsp tamarind juice
I green chilli, chopped
15 g/½ oz fresh ginger, finely grated
I onion, finely chopped
¼ tsp turmeric

450 g/I lb fresh sardines, cleaned
salt
4–6 curry leaves

1 Heat half the oil in a pan, add the coriander seeds and red chilli and fry for 3–4 minutes until the fragrance emerges, then grind, pound or blend with the coconut.

2 Return to the pan and continue to fry, adding the tamarind, green chilli, ginger, half the onion and the turmeric, for a further 5–7 minutes, until they make a thick paste.

3 Lay the sardines on a plate, smother them in the paste and leave to marinate for 15 minutes.

4 Meanwhile, heat the remaining oil and fry the remaining onion until golden.

5 Add the marinated sardines to the pan with 2 tbsp water, cover

Above Fried spiced fish/
Machi masala

and cook on a low heat for 5–8 minutes, until tender.

6 Add salt to taste and sprinkle on the curry leaves.

Photograph on page 124.

Prawn Biriyani
(Jhinga biriyani)

SERVES 4

Prawns

1 green chilli

15 g/½ oz fresh ginger, grated

1 clove garlic, chopped

50 g/2 oz grated or desiccated
coconut

4 cashew nuts

2 tsp biriyani masala

50 g/2 oz butter or ghee

1 small onion, chopped

450 g/1 lb shelled prawns

salt

1 tbsp lemon juice

cashew nuts and sultanas, fried in a
little butter or ghee, for
decoration

Rice

50 g/2 oz butter or ghee

1 small onion, chopped

2 bay leaves

225 g/8 oz basmati rice, washed,
soaked in water for 20 minutes
and drained

salt

100 g/4 oz fresh peas

1 Grind, pound or blend in a liquidizer the chilli, ginger, garlic, coconut, cashews and biriyani masala to make a thick paste.

2 Heat the butter or ghee in a pan, add the onion and fry until golden.

3 Add the blended spice paste and fry for a further 5–8 minutes, stirring.

4 Add the prawns and ½ tsp salt and cook on a low heat for 3–4 minutes, stirring, until the prawns

are hot through and coated in the spice mixture.

5 For the rice, heat the butter or ghee in a pan, add the onion and bay leaves and fry until the onion turns golden.

6 Pour on the rice, stir and fry for about 10 minutes, until translucent.

7 Add ½ tsp salt, the peas and enough water to cover and simmer on a low heat for 10–15 minutes, until the rice is almost cooked.

8 Stir the prawns and rice together in an ovenproof casserole, cover with a lid or foil and cook in the oven at 150°C/300°F/Gas 2 for 10–15 minutes.

9 Sprinkle over the lemon juice, cashews and sultanas and add extra salt to taste.

Above Prawn biriyani/Jhinga biriyani

Above Prawn vindaloo/
Jhinga vindaloo

Prawn Vindaloo
(*Jhinga vindaloo*)

SERVES 4

½ tsp cumin seeds
25 g/1 oz fresh ginger, finely grated
1–2 cloves garlic, finely chopped
1 tsp mustard seeds
3 tbsp oil
2 onions, finely chopped
6 curry leaves
100 g/4 oz tomatoes, peeled and
    chopped
2 tsp chilli powder
½ tsp turmeric
450 g/1 lb shelled prawns (or
    langoustines)
3 tbsp white wine vinegar
1 tsp cornflour (optional)
salt
½ tsp sugar (optional)

1 Crush the cumin seeds with the ginger, garlic and mustard seeds.

2 Heat the oil in a pan, add the onion and curry leaves and fry until the onion is golden.

3 Add the tomato, chilli powder, turmeric and 1–2 tbsp water and cook, mashing the tomato under the back of a wooden spoon to make a thick paste.

4 Add the crushed spices and continue to fry for 5 minutes, then add the prawns and 4 tbsp water and simmer for 10 minutes.

5 Pour on the vinegar. The sauce may be thickened, if necessary, by adding the cornflour mixed with 1 tsp water. Add salt to taste and sugar, if liked.

Fish Cooked in Coconut Milk
(*Mouli*)

SERVES 4
700 g/1 ½ lb white fish, cleaned
50 g/2 oz creamed coconut
250 ml/8 fl oz boiling water
4 tbsp oil
3 cloves
1 medium onion, finely chopped
¼ tsp ground turmeric
1 tsp salt
3–4 green chillies
6–8 curry leaves

1 Cut the fish into 8–10 equal sized pieces.

2 Blend together the creamed coconut and the boiling water in a blender or food processor until smooth.

3 Heat the oil over a medium heat and fry the pieces of fish, a few at a time, until lightly browned. Keep on one side.

4 Add the cloves to the remaining oil. When they swell up, add the onion and fry until lightly golden. Add the turmeric and salt and stir fry for a few seconds.

5 Add the fish gently and mix.

6 Add the coconut milk and, when it starts to boil, cover, lower the heat to medium low and cook for about 10–12 minutes.

7 Add the chillies and curry leaves and cook for a further couple of minutes until the fish is tender. Serve hot with rice.
This dish can be also made with prawns.

Below Spiced prawns/Jhinga batana

Fish in a Yoghurt Sauce
(Dahi mach)

SERVES 4
700 g/1½ lb white fish, cleaned and
    cut into 2.5 cm/1 in pieces.
1½ tsp salt
4 tbsp ghee (see page 21)
4 cardamom pods
5 cm/2 in cinnamon stick
2 bay leaves
1 medium onion, finely sliced
2 cm/¾ in ginger, grated
1 tbsp raisins
2–3 green chillies
about 120 ml/4 fl oz }   lightly
    natural yoghurt }   whisked
    175 ml/6 fl oz water }   together
    ½ tsp sugar

1 Sprinkle ½ tsp of salt on the fish and rub into the pieces.

2 Heat the ghee in a karai or saucepan over a medium high heat, and gently fry the pieces of fish, a few at a time, until lightly golden. Put aside.

3 In the remaining ghee, add the cardamom, cinnamon and bay leaves and let them sizzle for 3–4 seconds.

4 Add the onion, ginger and raisins and fry, stirring constantly, until the onion is golden.

5 Add the chillies, yoghurt and water mixture, sugar and the remaining salt and bring to a boil. Gently add the pieces of fish. Cover, lower the heat and cook for 15–20 minutes until the fish is cooked and the gravy slightly thickened.

Spiced Prawns
(Jhinga batana)

SERVES 4
450 g/1 lb prawns
1½ tsp salt
½ tsp ground turmeric
4 cloves garlic
2 cm/¾ in ginger
4 green chillies
6 tbsp oil
2 medium onions, finely chopped
1½ tsp ground coriander
1½ tsp ground cumin
175 ml/6 fl oz water
175 g/6 oz peas
1 tsp molasses or brown sugar
2 tbsp tamarind juice (see page 22)
2 tbsp chopped coriander leaves
2 tbsp grated coconut

1 Shell the prawns, leaving the tails on. Make a small cut along the back to remove the black vein. Wash the prawns and rub in ½ tsp of the salt and turmeric. Put aside for 1 hour.

2 Grind the garlic, ginger and green chillies to a paste.

3 In a large saucepan, heat the oil and fry the onions until lightly golden.

4 Add the prawns and paste and stir fry for 2–3 minutes.

5 Add the coriander, cumin and remaining salt, and continue to fry for a further minute.

6 Add the water, bring to the boil, reduce the heat to medium low, cover and simmer for 10 minutes.

7 Add the peas, molasses or sugar and tamarind juice, cover again and cook for about 20 minutes until the prawns are tender. Garnish with the coriander leaves and coconut.

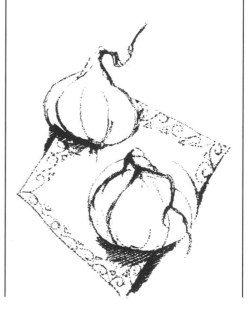

Prawns in a Coconut Sauce
(*Chingre macher malai*)

SERVES 4
450 g/1 lb Dublin Bay prawns
1½ tsp ground turmeric
1½ tsp salt
50 g/2 oz creamed coconut
300 ml/½ pt hot water
120 ml/4 fl oz oil
2 medium potatoes, peeled and
   quartered
1 large onion, finely sliced
½ tsp chilli powder
½ tsp sugar
2–3 green chillies

1 Shell the prawns, leaving the tails on. Make a small cut along the back to remove the black vein. Wash and pat dry. Rub ½ tsp each of turmeric and salt into the prawns.

Fish in a Hot Sauce
(*Macher jhal*)

SERVES 4
700 g/1½ lb white fish, cleaned
1½ tsp ground turmeric
1½ tsp salt
120 ml/4 fl oz oil
1 large onion, finely sliced
½ tsp chilli powder
250 ml/4 fl oz water
2–3 green chillies

1 Cut the fish into 8–10 equal-sized pieces.

2 Rub ½ tsp each of turmeric and salt into the fish.

3 Heat the oil in a karai or saucepan over a medium high heat and fry the pieces of fish, a few at a time, until lightly browned. Put aside.

4 In the remaining oil, fry the onion until brown. Add the remaining turmeric, salt and chilli powder and stir fry for a further 1 minute.

5 Add the water and bring to the boil; gently add the pieces of fish and the green chillies. Cover, lower the heat to medium and cook for about 15 minutes until the fish is cooked and the gravy thickened.

Above .Fish in a hot sauce/
Macher jhal

Right Prawns in a coconut sauce/
Chingre macher malai

2 In a food processor or liquidizer, blend together the creamed coconut and water. Put aside.

3 Heat the oil in a saucepan and fry the potatoes until evenly browned. Put aside.

4 Add the prawns and fry until golden. Put aside.

5 Add the onion to the remaining oil and fry until golden brown. Add the remaining turmeric, salt, chilli powder and sugar and fry for 1–2 minutes with the onion.

6 Add the blended coconut milk and bring to the boil. Add the prawns and green chillies.

7 Cover, lower the heat and cook for 10 minutes. Add the potatoes, cover again and cook for a further 20–25 minutes, until the prawns are cooked and the gravy thickened.

Fish Curry
(*Macher kalia*)

Above Fish curry/Macher kalia

SERVES 4
700 g/1 ½ lb white fish, cleaned
1 ½ tsp ground turmeric
1 ½ tsp salt
1 medium onion, quartered
2 cloves garlic
2 cm/¾ in ginger
1 tbsp vinegar
8 tbsp oil
2 medium potatoes, peeled and
   quartered
4 cardamom pods
2 × 2.5 cm/1 in cinnamon stick
2 bay leaves
½ tsp chilli powder
¼ tsp sugar
300 ml/½ pt water
3–4 green chillies

1 Cut the fish into 8–10 equal-sized pieces.

2 Rub ½ tsp each of turmeric and salt into the fish.

3 In a food processor or liquidizer, blend together the onion, garlic, ginger and vinegar.

4 Heat the oil in a karai or saucepan and fry the potatoes, turning often, until evenly browned. Put aside.

5 Gently add a few pieces of fish and fry until golden. Put aside.

6 In the remaining oil, add the cardamom, cinnamon and bay leaves and let them sizzle for 5–6 seconds.

7 Add the blended mixture and, stirring constantly, fry until golden brown.

8 Add the remaining turmeric, salt, chilli powder and sugar, mix thoroughly with the onion mixture and fry for 1–2 minutes.

9 Add the water and green chillies and bring to the boil. Add the pieces of potato and fish. Cover, lower the heat and cook for 15–20 minutes until the potatoes are tender. Serve with rice.

Madras Pepper Crab
(*Mandaraj mulaku nandoo*)

SERVES 2
150 ml/¼ pt oil
3 medium onions, finely sliced
1 large cooked crab, cut into pieces
1½ tbsp coarsely ground black
   pepper
1½ tsp salt

1 Heat the oil and fry the onions until soft and transparent.

2 Add the pieces of crab and fry with the onions for 3–4 minutes.

3 Add the pepper and salt and continue to fry for 8–10 minutes until cooked. Serve with plain rice.

Below Madras pepper crab/
Mandaraj mulaku nandoo

Above Steamed prawns/
Bhape chingre

Steamed Prawns
(Bhape chingre)

SERVES 2

450 g/1 lb Dublin Bay prawns
1 tsp ground turmeric
½ tsp chilli powder
1 tsp black mustard seeds, ground
2–3 green chillies
1 tsp salt
2 tbsp oil

1 Shell the prawns, leaving the tails on. Make a small cut down the back to remove the black vein. Wash and pat dry.

2 Thoroughly mix all the ingredients with the prawns. Place the mixture in a bowl (half fill it only), and tie a double thickness of aluminum foil around the top of the bowl.

3 In a large saucepan, boil some water and place the bowl of prawns in the saucepan, so that the water reaches a quarter of the way up the bowl.

4 Cover the saucepan, lower the heat and keep boiling, topping up the boiling water during cooking as necessary. Steam for about 30–40 minutes.

Eggs

. . . .

Eggs can be used to make a very quick and satisfying curry. Hard-boiled eggs can be shelled and pierced with the point of a sharp knife to let in the flavours of the sauce they are being cooked in. Curried scrambled eggs make a very speedy lunch for one, as well as an unusual side dish at dinner.

Egg Curry
(*Undey ki curry*)

SERVES 4
4 tbsp oil
1 large onion, finely sliced
2 tbsp onion mixture (see page 22)
½ tsp ground turmeric
½ tsp chilli powder
¾ tsp salt
a big pinch of sugar
8 hard-boiled eggs
120 ml/4 fl oz water

1 Heat the oil in a frying pan over medium high heat and fry the sliced onion for 3–4 minutes until lightly browned.

2 Add the onion mixture, turmeric, chilli, salt and sugar and, stirring constantly, fry for another 2–3 minutes. Add the eggs and mix until well covered with the spices.

3 Add the water, bring to the boil, lower the heat, cover and cook for about 10 minutes until the gravy thickens.

Curried Eggs
(*Undey ki*)

SERVES 4–6
3–4 tbsp oil
2 small onions, grated
15 g/½ oz fresh ginger, grated
2 cloves garlic, crushed
2.5 cm/1 in cinnamon stick
1 bay leaf
½ tsp chilli powder
2 tbsp ground coriander
2 cashew nuts, ground
225 g/8 oz tomatoes, peeled and chopped
120 ml/¼ pt water
salt
6 hard-boiled eggs
½ tsp garam masala
leaves from 1 sprig of coriander
1 tsp lemon juice
4 peppercorns, crushed

1 Heat the oil in a pan, add the onion, ginger, garlic, cinnamon and bay leaf and fry until the onion is golden.

2 Add the chilli powder, ground coriander, cashew and tomato and continue to cook, mashing the tomato under the back of a wooden spoon to make a thick paste.

3 Pour on the water with ½ tsp salt, bring to the boil and add the eggs. Cook over a low heat for 5 minutes.

4 Take the curry off the heat and sprinkle on the garam masala, coriander leaves, lemon juice and pepper. Add extra salt to taste.

Opposite Egg curry/Undey ki curry

Above Fried egg curry/
Masala undey

Fried Egg Curry
(Masala undey)

SERVES 4
3 medium onions
5 cloves garlic
2.5 cm/1 in ginger
1 tbsp white vinegar
8 tbsp mustard oil
8 eggs
3 bay leaves
5 cm/2 in cinnamon stick
6 cardamoms
2–3 green chillies
1½ tsp ground turmeric
½ tsp chilli powder
1 tsp salt
¼ tsp sugar

1 Blend the onions, garlic, ginger and vinegar in a blender until you have a fine paste.

2 Heat the oil in a large frying pan over a medium heat, fry the eggs one at a time and set aside.

3 To the remaining oil add the bay leaves, cinnamon and cardamoms and let them sizzle for a few seconds.

4 Add the blended paste and the green chillies and fry for 6–8 minutes, stirring constantly. Add the turmeric, chilli powder, salt and sugar and continue frying for another minute.

5 Carefully add the eggs and, stirring gently, cover them with some of the spices.

6 Cover and cook for 5 minutes. Serve hot with a pillau (see rice dishes).

Devilled Eggs
(*Undey ka devil*)

SERVES 2

4 hard-boiled eggs, cut in half
   lengthways
1½ tbsp onions, finely chopped
2 green chillies, finely chopped
1 tbsp coriander leaves, chopped
½ tsp salt
2 tbsp mashed potatoes
oil for deep frying
1 tbsp plain flour
50 ml/2 fl oz water

1 Separate the eggs and mix the yolks with the onions, chillies, coriander leaves, salt and mashed potatoes. Put the mixture back into the egg whites. Chill for 30 minutes.

2 Heat the oil in a karai over high heat. While the oil is heating up make a batter with the flour and water. Be careful not to allow the oil to catch fire.

3 Dip the eggs into the batter and gently put into the hot oil. Fry until golden, turning once.

Below Devilled eggs/Undey ka devil

140

Omelette Curry

SERVES 4
6 eggs
½ tsp salt
6 tbsp oil
I large potato, cut into 2.5 cm/I in pieces
4 tbsp onion mixture (see page 22)
I tsp ground turmeric
½ tsp chilli powder
¾ tsp salt
350 ml/12 fl oz water

1 Whisk the eggs and the salt together.

2 Heat 1 tbsp of the oil in a large frying pan and make an omelette with half the beaten eggs. Set aside and cut into four pieces. Similarly, make another omelette.

3 Heat the rest of the oil and fry the potatoes until lightly browned. Set aside. Add the onion mixture and fry for 2–3 minutes. Add the turmeric, chilli and salt and stir well with the onion mixture.

4 Add the water and bring to the boil. Put in the potatoes, cover, lower the heat and simmer for 10 minutes. Place the pieces of omelette in the pan, cover again and cook until the potatoes are tender, about another 10 minutes.

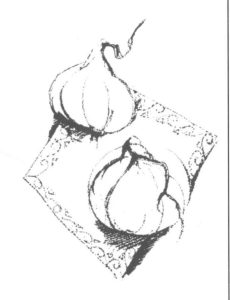

Below Omelette curry

Whole Eggs Fried with Spice
(Undey masala)

SERVES 4
6 hard-boiled eggs
2 tbsp oil
2 tsp ground coriander
I tsp chilli powder
¼ tsp ground pepper
salt
2 tbsp lemon juice

1 Make several cuts into the eggs with the point of a sharp knife to allow the spices to enter.

2 Heat the oil, add the coriander, chilli powder, pepper and salt and fry for about 3 minutes.

3 Add the lemon juice and stir to make a paste.

4 Add the eggs to the pan and turn in the paste to coat. Continue cooking, turning occasionally, for 4–5 minutes.

Yellow Rice with Hard-boiled Eggs
(*Unday ki biriyani*)

SERVES 4–6
300–350 g/10–12 oz basmati rice
100 g/4 oz butter or ghee
1 small onion, chopped
2 cloves garlic, chopped
1 green chilli, chopped
cardamom seeds from 2 pods
2 bay leaves
3 cloves
600 ml/1 pt boiling water
salt
½ tsp turmeric
1 chicken stock cube, optional
10–15 cashew nuts
50 g/2 oz ghee
25 g/1 oz sultanas
4–6 hard-boiled eggs
1 tsp lemon juice

1 Wash the rice thoroughly in 2 or 3 changes of water, then soak for 10–15 minutes.

2 Heat the butter or ghee in a pan, add the onion, garlic, green chilli, cardamom seeds, bay leaves and cloves, and fry until the onion is golden.

3 Drain the rice, pour it into the pan, stir and fry for 10 minutes, until it turns translucent.

4 Pour on the boiling water, add ½ tsp salt, the turmeric and the stock cube, and simmer over a low heat for 10 minutes. Turn off the heat and leave, covered, for 5 minutes until all the moisture has been absorbed and the grains of rice are separate and tender.

5 Fry the cashew nuts for a couple of minutes in the ghee, adding the sultanas for the last few seconds.

6 Cut the eggs in half, sprinkle with lemon juice and rub with salt.

7 Spread the rice in a serving dish, sprinkle with salt to taste and arrange the eggs, cashew nuts and sultanas on top.

Scrambled Eggs with Onion
(*Piyaz ekuri*)

SERVES 2
1 small onion, finely chopped
1 tsp chilli powder
2 curry leaves

Above Yellow rice with hard-boiled eggs/Undey ki biriyani

2 eggs, beaten
salt
1–2 tbsp oil

1 Pound, grind, or blend in a liquidizer the onion, chilli powder and curry leaves, then mix with the beaten egg and ½ tsp salt.

2 Heat the oil in a pan, add the eggs and cook gently, stirring, until scrambled, for about 2 minutes. (The eggs will continue to cook after you have removed them from the heat, so be careful not to overcook.)

Spiced Scrambled Egg
(Ekuri)

SERVES 2
2 eggs
1 small onion, finely chopped
1 green chilli, finely chopped
2 curry leaves
15 g/½ oz fresh ginger, finely grated
2 tbsp oil
salt

1 Beat the eggs well.

2 Stir together the onion, chilli, curry leaves and ginger.

3 Heat the oil in a pan, add the onion mixture and fry for 3 minutes, stirring.

4 Add the eggs and cook gently, stirring, for about 2 minutes, until scrambled. (The eggs will continue cooking after you take them from the heat, so be careful not to overcook.) Add salt to taste.

Scrambled Eggs with Mushrooms and Prawns
(Jhinga kumban ekuri)

SERVES 2
2 tbsp oil
1 small onion, finely chopped
75 g/3 oz mushrooms, peeled and
    sliced
75 g/3 oz peeled prawns
15 g/½ oz fresh ginger, finely grated
1 green chilli, finely chopped
75 g/3 oz tomatoes, peeled and
    chopped
2 curry leaves
3 eggs, beaten
salt

1 Heat the oil in a pan, add the onion and fry until golden.

2 Add the mushrooms, prawns, ginger, green chilli, tomato and curry leaves and fry, stirring, for 5 minutes.

3 Add the eggs with ½ tsp salt and cook gently, stirring, for about 3 minutes, to scramble. (The eggs will continue to cook after you take them from the heat, so be careful not to overcook.)

Right Scrambled eggs with mushrooms and prawns/Jhinga kumban ekuri

Bread

· ·

Breads can be fried or grilled. An ordinary gas or electric oven can be used to grill the various breads, but for best results a Tandoor should be used. This is a barrel-shaped clay oven which gives breads that special charcoal flavour. Try grilling breads on a barbecue and see how your friends react.

Indians eat these breads with their fingers. Tear a piece of bread and dip it into a plate of curry or wrap a small piece of bread around a dry vegetable. And don't forget to lick your fingers!

Wholewheat Unleavened Bread
(Chappati)

275 g/10 oz wholewheat flour
½ tsp salt
about 175 ml/6 fl oz hot water
3 tbsp melted ghee (see page 21)

1 Sieve the flour and salt together. Add enough water to form a soft dough.

2 Knead for about 10 minutes until no longer sticky. Cover and set aside for 1 hour.

3 Divide the dough into 12–14 balls. On a floured surface roll each ball into 15 cm/6 in rounds.

4 Preheat the grill to very hot.

5 Heat a frying pan over medium heat and place a chappati on it. Cook the chappati for 2 minutes until brown spots appear. Turn and cook the other side in the same way.

6 Take the chappati and place it under the hot grill for a few seconds; it will puff up. Turn and cook the other side for a few seconds until it also puffs up.

7 Place the chappati in a dish and brush with a little melted ghee. Cover and keep warm while cooking the others.

Below Wholewheat unleavened bread/Chappati

Layered Bread
(*Paratha*)

350 g/12 oz plain flour
½ tsp salt
4 tbsp oil
about 175 ml/6 fl oz hot water
3 heaped tbsp melted ghee (see
    page 21)

1 Sieve the flour and salt together. Rub in the oil.

2 Slowly add the water to form a soft dough. Knead for about 10 minutes until it is no longer sticky.

3 Divide the dough into 16 balls. Flatten a dough ball on a lightly floured surface with your hand and then roll into a 20 cm/8 in circle.

4 Brush a little ghee on this and fold in half, brush on a little more ghee and fold into a small triangle. Roll out the triangle quite thinly on the floured surface.

5 Heat a frying pan over medium heat and place a rolled triangle on it. Heat each side for 1 minute until brown specks appear. Keep aside. Cook each triangle in this manner.

6 Add the ghee and gently fry the parathas one at a time for 1–2 minutes, turning once, until golden brown. (While cooking the parathas, keep the fried parathas warm by wrapping in foil).

Below Layered bread/Paratha

Deep Fried White Bread
(*Lucchi*)

350 g/12 oz plain flour
½ tsp salt
2 tbsp oil
about 175 ml/6 fl oz hot water
oil for deep frying

1 Sieve the flour and salt together. Rub in the oil.

2 Slowly add enough water to form a stiff dough. Knead for about 10 minutes until you have a soft, pliable dough.

3 Divide the dough into about 40 small balls and flatten each ball.

4 Roll out a few balls on a slightly oily surface into rounds of 10 cm/ 4 in across (do not roll out all the balls at the same time as they tend to stick).

5 Heat the oil in a karai over high heat. Put in a lucchi and press the middle with a slotted spoon as this causes the lucchi to puff up. Turn and cook the other side for a few seconds. Drain and serve hot.

Cornmeal Bread
(*Makki ki roti*)

300 g/11 oz coarse cornmeal
pinch of salt
about 120 ml/4 fl oz hot water
melted butter

1 Sieve the flour and salt together.

2 Add enough water to make a stiff dough. Knead with your palms for about 10 minutes until soft and smooth.

3 Divide the dough into 8–10 balls.

4 Take one of the balls and place it on a lightly floured surface and, with the palm of your hand, press the ball gently to about 13 cm/5 in diameter and less than 5 mm/¼ in thick. (If the dough tends to stick in your hand place a little flour on top of the dough.)

5 Gently lift out the roti and place on a hot tava or frying pan and cook until golden. Turn and cook the other side in the same way.

6 Pierce the roti a few times with a fork, and brush with the melted butter. Do all the rotis in the same way. Serve with Spicy mustard leaves (see page 63).

Below Deep fried white bread/ Lucchi

Above Leavened bread/Naan

Leavened Bread
(Naan)

1 tsp dried yeast
1 tsp sugar
75 ml/3 fl oz lukewarm water
275 g/10 oz plain flour
½ tsp salt
¾ tsp baking powder
1 tbsp oil
about 3 tbsp plain yoghurt

1 Stir the yeast and sugar into the water and set aside for 15–20 minutes until the liquid is frothy.

2 Sieve together the flour, salt and baking powder. Make a well in the middle, add the yeast liquid, oil and yoghurt and knead for about 10 minutes till soft and no longer sticky.

3 Place the dough in an oiled plastic bag and set aside in a warm place for 2–3 hours until double in size.

4 Preheat the oven to 200°C/ 400°F/Gas 6. Knead the dough again for 1–2 minutes and divide into 12 balls. Roll into 18 cm/7 in rounds.

5 Place as many as possible on a baking sheet and put in the oven for 4–5 minutes each side until brown spots appear. Place them for a few seconds under a hot grill until slightly browned.

6 Wrap the cooked ones in foil while cooking the others.

Yoghurt Bread
(Batora)

225 g/8 oz plain flour
1½ tsp baking powder
½ tsp salt
1 tsp sugar
1 egg, beaten
about 3 tbsp yoghurt
oil for deep frying

1 Sieve the flour, baking powder and salt together. Mix in the sugar.

2 Add the beaten egg and enough yoghurt to form a stiff dough. Knead for 10–15 minutes until you have a soft, smooth dough. Cover with a cloth and let it rest for 3–4 hours.

3 Knead again on a floured surface for 5 minutes. Divide into 12–14 balls.

4 Roll out on a floured surface into 12.5 cm/5 in rounds.

5 Heat the oil in a karai over high heat. Fry the batora, pressing in the middle with a slotted spoon so that it puffs up. Turn and cook the other side for a few seconds until lightly browned. Drain. Serve hot with Curried chick peas or Soured chick peas (see pages 51, 50).

Below Yoghurt bread/Batora

Stuffed Deep Fried Bread
(Mater kachori)

Filling
1 tbsp ghee (see page 21)
pinch of asafoetida
5 mm/¾ in root ginger, grated
225 g/8 oz peas, boiled and mashed
¼ tsp chilli powder
¼ tsp salt
½ tsp garam masala (see page 13)
Dough
225 g/8 oz plain flour
½ tsp salt
1½ tsp ghee
approx 120 ml/4 fl oz hot water
oil for deep frying

1 To make the filling, heat the ghee in a karai over medium heat, add the asafoetida and ginger and fry for a few seconds.

2 Add the mashed peas, chilli and salt and, stirring constantly, fry for about 5 minutes until the mixture leaves the sides and forms a ball. Mix in the garam masala and set aside to cool.

3 To make the dough, sieve the flour and salt together. Rub in the ghee. Add enough water to make a stiff dough. Knead for about 10 minutes to form a soft pliable dough. Divide into 20 balls.

4 Insert your thumb into the middle of each ball to form a cup. Fill with 1 tsp of the filling. Seal the top and make it into a ball again.

5 Flatten and roll into 10 cm/4 in rounds on a slightly oiled surface (take care that no holes appear when rolling).

6 Heat the oil in a karai until very hot. Gently put in a kachori and press the middle so that it puffs up. Turn and fry the other side until lightly golden. Drain on paper towels and serve hot with Potato masala curry (see page 76).

Right Stuffed deep fried bread/
Mater kachori

Deep Fried Brown Bread
(*Poori*)

225 g/8 oz wholewheat flour
½ tsp salt
2 tbsp oil
about 90 ml/3 ½ oz hot water
oil for deep frying

1 Sieve together with flour and salt. Rub in the oil. Add enough water to make a stiff dough.

2 Put the dough on a floured surface and knead for about 10 minutes till soft and smooth.

3 Divide the mixture into 20 balls.

4 Take one ball at a time, flatten it on a slightly oiled surface and roll into rounds of 10 cm/4 in across. (Do not stack the rolled pooris on one another as they might stick together.)

5 Heat the oil in a karai until very hot and add a poori, pressing the middle with a slotted spoon so that it puffs up. Quickly turn and cook the other side for a few seconds. Drain and serve hot.

Left Deep fried brown bread/ Poori

Stuffed Layered Bread
(*Aloo paratha*)

Filling

450 g/1 lb potatoes, boiled and
mashed
1 small onion, finely chopped
1–2 green chillies, finely chopped
1 tbsp chopped coriander leaves
¾ tsp salt
¾ tsp ground roasted cumin
(see page 23)

Dough

350 g/12 oz plain flour
½ tsp salt
4 tbsp oil
about 175 ml/6 fl oz hot water
ghee (see page 21) for frying

1 To make the filling, mix all the ingredients together and set aside.

2 To make the dough, sieve the flour and salt together. Rub in the oil. Add enough water to form a stiff dough. Knead for about 10 minutes until you have a smooth dough. Divide into 20 balls.

3 Roll out two balls into 10 cm/ 4 in rounds each. Place about 1½– 2 tbsp of the filling on one of the rounds and spread it evenly. Place the other round over the filling, sealing the edges with a little water.

4 Roll out gently into 18 cm/7 in rounds, taking care that no filling comes out. Roll out all the parathas in a similar manner.

5 Heat a frying pan over medium heat. Place a paratha in the frying pan and cook for about 1 minute until brown spots appear. Turn and cook the other side.

6 Add 2 tsp of ghee and cook for 2–3 minutes until golden brown. Turn and cook the other side, adding more ghee if required. Make all the parathas in the same way. Serve warm.

Below Stuffed layered bread/
Aloo paratha

Rice

· ·

The "King of Rice" is the basmati variety that comes from Dehra Dun – one of the hill stations founded by the British as a summer retreat. This rice carries a unique flavour when cooked and is by far the best quality. Other types of rice are Pakistani basmati rice, patna rice and tilds rice. American long-grain rice is also adequate for the preparation of Indian meals.

Plain Rice I
(*Sada chawal I*)

SERVES 4
350 g/12 oz basmati rice
900 ml/1 ½ pt cold water

1 Rinse the rice three or four times in cold water. Drain.

2 Place the drained rice in a large saucepan and pour in the measured amount of water. Bring it to the boil rapidly over a high heat. Stir.

3 Lower the heat to very low, cover and cook for about 20 minutes until all the water has evaporated.

4 Fluff the rice with a fork and serve hot.

Plain Rice II
(*Sada chawal II*)

SERVES 4
350 g/12 oz basmati rice
2.75 litres/5 pt cold water

1 Rinse the rice in cold water three or four times. Soak the rice in 1.6 litres/3 pt water for 1 hour. Drain.

2 Place the drained rice in a large saucepan, add the 2.75 litres/5 pt water. Bring to the boil over high heat and boil rapidly for 5 minutes until the rice is cooked. Drain the rice, fluff it with a fork and serve hot.

Fried Rice
(*Ghee bhat*)

SERVES 4
3 tbsp ghee (see page 21)
2 bay leaves
5 cm/2 in cinnamon stick
4 cardamoms
3 large onions, finely sliced
3 green chillies, cut lengthwise
350 g/12 oz basmati rice, cooked and cooled
1 tsp salt
½ tsp sugar
2 tbsp raisins (optional)

1 Heat the ghee in a large frying pan over medium high heat. Add the bay leaves, cinnamon and cardamoms and let them sizzle for a few seconds.

2 Add the onions and chillies and fry until the onions are golden brown.

3 Add the rice, salt, sugar and raisins and continue frying until the rice is thoroughly heated up.

Opposite Fried rice/Ghee bhat

Lemon Rice
(*Nimbowala chawal*)

SERVES 4
275–350 g/10–12 oz cooked
    basmati rice
2 tbsp lemon juice
¼ tsp asafoetida
½ tsp turmeric
salt
2 tbsp oil
½ tsp mustard seeds
1 tsp polished split black lentils (urid
    dal)
6 curry leaves
2 tbsp split gram, soaked in water for
    20 minutes, then drained
15 g/½ oz fresh ginger, finely grated
1 green chilli, chopped

1 Mix the rice with the lemon juice, asafoetida, turmeric and salt to taste.

2 Heat the oil in a pan, add the mustard seeds, dal, curry leaves and split gram and fry until all the mustard seeds have popped.

3 Add the ginger, green chilli and rice and heat through, stirring, for about 5 minutes, until hot.

4 Add extra salt to taste.

Tomato Rice
(*Tamatar chawal*)

SERVES 4
2 tbsp oil
½ tsp mustard seeds
2 tbsp split gram, soaked in water for
    20 minutes, then drained
6 curry leaves
1 red chilli, cut into pieces
1 onion, chopped
15 g/½ oz fresh ginger, finely grated
2 cloves garlic, sliced
1 green chilli, chopped
350 g/12 oz tomatoes, peeled and
    chopped
1 tsp sugar
275–350 g/10–12 oz cooked
    basmati rice
1 tsp ghee (see page 21)
salt

1 Heat the oil in a pan, add the mustard seeds, split gram, curry leaves and red chilli and fry until all the mustard seeds have popped and the gram is golden brown.

2 Add the onion, ginger, garlic and green chilli and fry for 3–5 minutes, stirring.

3 Add the tomato and sugar and cook, mashing the tomato under the back of a wooden spoon to make a thick paste.

4 Stir in the rice and ghee and heat through, stirring, for about 5 minutes until hot. Add extra salt to taste.

Above left Lemon rice/Nimbowala
chawal

Below Tomato rice/Tamatar chawal

Rice with Yoghurt
(*Dahi chawal*)

SERVES 4

225 g/8 oz yoghurt

275–350 g/10–12 oz cooked
    basmati rice

2 tbsp oil

2 tsp polished split black lentils (urid
    dal)

1 tsp mustard seeds

4–6 curry leaves

2 red or green chillies, chopped

salt

1 Mix the yoghurt into the rice,
without mashing the grains.

2 Heat the oil in a pan, add the dal
and fry until light brown.

3 Add the mustard seeds, curry
leaves and chilli and fry until all
the seeds have popped.

4 Stir the contents of the pan into
the rice, mixing carefully, and add
salt to taste.

Below Rice with yoghurt/
Dahi chawal

159

Spiced Rice
(*Masale bhat*)

SERVES 4
275 g/10 oz basmati rice
3 tsp coriander seeds
2 tsp cumin seeds
1 cm/½ in cinnamon stick
3 cardamom pods, shelled
2 cloves
3 tbsp oil
¾ tsp mustard seeds
good pinch of asafoetida
½ tsp ground turmeric
1 tsp chilli powder
1 small cauliflower, broken into large
    florets
750 ml/1¼ pt water
1½ tsp salt
3 tbsp chopped coriander leaves
3 tbsp grated coconut

1 Wash the rice in several changes of water and soak for 1 hour in plenty of water. Drain the rice and leave in a sieve for about 20 minutes.

2 While the rice is soaking, dry roast the coriander, cumin, cinnamon, cardamom and cloves over a medium heat, until they are a few shades darker and emit a rich aroma.

3 Grind the spices to a fine powder and put aside.

4 In a large saucepan, heat the oil, add the mustard seeds and let them sizzle for 5–6 seconds. Add the asafoetida, turmeric, chilli powder and cauliflower and, taking care not to burn the spices, stir fry for 1–2 minutes.

5 Add the rice and sauté for a few minutes, making sure that the rice does not become brown.

6 Add the water, bring to a boil, give it a good stir, lower the heat to very low, cover and cook for 8 minutes. Remove the cover, add the powdered spices and salt, mix, cover again and cook for a further 10 minutes until all the water is absorbed.

7 Fluff gently with a fork. Garnish with the coriander leaves and coconut. Serve hot with ghee.

Pillau with Coconut and Milk
(*Narial aur dudh pillau*)

SERVES 4
350 g/12 oz basmati rice, rinsed and
    drained
2 tbsp desiccated coconut
2–3 green chillies
1 tsp salt
½ tsp sugar
2 tbsp raisins
1 tbsp pistachio nuts, skinned and cut
    into thin strips
2 bay leaves
5 cm/2 in cinnamon stick
4 cardamoms
3 tbsp ghee (see page 21)
600 ml/1 pt milk
300 ml/½ pt water

1 Mix the rice with the coconut, chillies, salt, sugar, raisins, pistachios, bay leaves, cinnamon and cardamoms.

2 Heat the ghee in a large saucepan over medium heat. Add the rice mixture and sauté for 5 minutes, stirring constantly.

3 Add the milk and water, increase the heat to high and bring it to the boil. Stir.

4 Lower the heat to very low, cover and cook for about 20 minutes until all the liquid has evaporated. Fluff the pillau with a fork and serve hot.

Rice and Lentil Curry
(Khichuri 1)

SERVES 3-4
225 g/8 oz basmati rice, washed and
    drained
50 g/2 oz moong dal, washed and
    drained
750 ml/1 ¼ pt water
1 ½ tbsp ghee (see page 21)

1 Mix the rice and dal and soak in plenty of water for 1 hour. Drain.

2 Add the rice and dal mixture to the measured water in a large saucepan and bring to the boil over a high heat. Turn the heat down to very low, cover and cook for about 20 minutes until all the water has been absorbed. Remove from the heat.

3 In a small pan, heat the ghee until very hot and pour it over the cooked rice and dal. Mix. Serve hot with Spinach with lentils and vegetables (see page 64), yoghurt and poppadum.

Left Pillau with coconut and milk/
Narial aur dudh pillau

Potato Pillau
(Aloo pillau)

SERVES 4–6
75 g/3 oz creamed coconut
600 ml/1 pt hot water
handful coriander leaves
1 tbsp shredded coconut
2 green chillies
2 tbsp lemon juice
½ tsp sugar
1½ tsp salt
½ tsp garam masala (see page 13)
¼ tsp ground turmeric
10–12 small new potatoes, washed
    and peeled
3 tbsp oil
2 cloves
1 medium onion, finely sliced
1 clove garlic, crushed
275 g/10 oz basmati rice, washed and
    drained

1 Make the coconut milk by blending together the creamed coconut and hot water. Put aside.

2 Chop the coriander leaves and throw away the lower stalks and roots. Wash them thoroughly.

3 Blend together the coriander leaves, shredded coconut, chillies, lemon juice, sugar, ½ tsp salt, garam masala and turmeric until you have a fine paste.

4 Parboil the potatoes. Drain and cool.

5 Take a potato and make 2 cuts like a cross coming about three quarters of the way down the length. Take care not to cut right through. Cut all the potatoes in this way.

6 Fill each potato with a little of the coriander paste. If you have any paste left, rub it on to the potatoes.

7 Heat the oil over a medium high heat in a large saucepan. Add the cloves, and, after 3–4 seconds, add the onion and garlic and fry until the onion is lightly golden.

8 Add the rice and sauté for 2–3 minutes, stirring constantly.

9 Add the coconut milk and 1 tsp salt and bring to a boil. Add the potatoes, and when it comes to the boil again, lower the heat to very low, cover and cook for about 20 minutes until all the water has been absorbed.

10 Fluff the rice with a fork before serving.

Rice with Lentils
(Khichuri II)

SERVES 4
75 g/3 oz moong dal
75 g/3 oz red lentils, washed
6 tbsp oil
2 bay leaves
5 cm/2 in cinnamon stick
4 cardamoms
3 cloves garlic, crushed
2.5 cm/1 in root ginger, grated
1 large onion, finely sliced
1 tsp ground turmeric
½ tsp chilli powder
1 tsp salt
⅓ tsp sugar
1 tomato, chopped
75 g/3 oz basmati rice, washed and
    drained
1.25 litres/2¼ pt water
3–4 green chillies, halved lengthwise

1 In a small pan dry roast the moong dal over medium heat, until it turns light brown. Remove from the heat, wash thoroughly, and mix with the red lentils. Put in a sieve to drain.

2 Heat the oil in a large saucepan over medium heat. Add the bay leaves, cinnamon stick and cardamoms and let them sizzle for a few seconds.

3 Add the garlic, ginger and onion and fry until the onion is golden brown.

4 Add the turmeric, chilli, salt, sugar and tomato and mix thoroughly. Add the rice and the lentils and continue to fry for 5–7 minutes.

5 Add the water, and when it starts to boil, lower the heat and simmer for about 35–40 minutes.

6 Just before removing from the heat, add the chillies. Serve with melted ghee (see page 21) and pakoras (see page 178).

Right Rice with lentils/Khichuri

Vegetable Pillau
(*Sabzi ka pillau*)

SERVES 4–6

275 g/10 oz basmati rice
5 tbsp ghee (see page 21)
2 tbsp unsalted cashew nuts
1 medium onion, finely chopped
1 cm/½ in ginger, cut into very thin
 strips
225 g/8 oz French beans, cut into
 4 cm/1½ in lengths
2 small carrots, scraped and diced
75 g/3 oz peas
1 small red pepper, seeded and
 thinly sliced
900 ml/1½ pt water
1½ tsp salt
1 tbsp coriander leaves

1 Wash the rice in several changes of water and leave in a sieve to drain thoroughly.

2 Heat the ghee in a large saucepan and fry the cashew nuts until golden. Drain and put aside.

3 In the remaining ghee, add the onion and ginger and fry until the onion is soft and transparent.

4 Add the rice and stir fry for 1–2 minutes. Add all the vegetables and mix with the onion and rice.

5 Add the water and salt and bring to a boil. Give it a good stir, lower the heat to very low, cover and cook for about 20 minutes until the rice and vegetables are tender and all the water is absorbed.

6 Garnish with the fried cashew nuts and coriander leaves.

Pea Pillau
(*Mater pillau*)

SERVES 4–6

3 tbsp oil
½ tsp whole cumin seeds
1 medium onion, finely chopped
100 g/4 oz peas
350 g/12 oz basmati rice, washed and
 drained
1 tsp salt
900 ml/1½ pt water

1 Heat the oil in a large saucepan over medium heat, add the cumin seeds and let them sizzle for a few seconds.

2 Add the onion and fry until soft. Add the peas, rice and salt and stir fry for about 5 minutes. Add the water and bring to the boil.

3 Cover tightly, lower the heat to very low and cook for about 20 minutes until all the water has been absorbed. Fluff the pillau with a fork and serve hot.

Mushroom Pillau
(*Khumbi pillau*)

SERVES 4–6
2 tbsp oil
2 bay leaves
5 cm/2 in cinnamon stick
4 cardamoms
1 large onion, finely chopped
175 g/6 oz mushrooms, sliced
350 g/12 oz basmati rice, washed and
    drained
1 tsp salt
900 ml/1 ½ pt water

1 Heat the oil in a large saucepan over medium high heat. Add the bay leaves, cinnamon and cardamoms and let them sizzle for a few seconds.

2 Add the onion and fry until soft. Add the mushrooms and fry for about 5 minutes until all the moisture has been absorbed.

3 Add the rice and salt and stir fry for 2–3 minutes. Add the water and bring to the boil.

4 Cover tightly, lower the heat to very low and cook for about 20 minutes until all the water has been absorbed. Fluff the pillau with a fork and serve hot.

Left Mushroom pillau/Khumbi pillau

Snacks and Salads

· ·

These recipes for snacks are extremely versatile. They are ideal for picnics as they can be eaten cold, served with a salad or chutney. They can also be served as a side dish with a main course, or alternatively, as an hors d'oeuvre.

Spicy Pounded Rice
(*Batata poha*)

SERVES 4

100 g/4 oz pounded rice
2 tbsp oil
½ tsp mustard seeds
1–2 dried red chillies, broken in half
1–2 green chillies, chopped
5–6 curry leaves
1 small onion, finely chopped
2 medium potatoes, boiled and diced
    into 1 cm/½ in cubes
¼ tsp ground turmeric
1 tsp salt
½ tsp chilli powder
2 tsp lime juice
2 tbsp coriander leaves, chopped

1 Wash the pounded rice and leave to drain in a sieve for about 15 minutes.

2 Heat the oil over a medium high heat and add the mustard seeds; as soon as they start to splutter add the red chillies, green chillies and curry leaves and let them sizzle for 7–8 seconds.

3 Add the onion and stir fry until golden.

4 Add the potatoes, turmeric, salt and chilli powder and mix with the onions.

5 Add the drained pounded rice and mix with the other ingredients; stir fry for 2–3 minutes.

6 Lower the heat, cover and cook for about 8–10 minutes, stirring occasionally (add a little extra oil if you think necessary).

7 Sprinkle on the lime juice and coriander leaves. Mix well and serve immediately. This is eaten for breakfast or as a light snack.

Savoury Puffed Rice
(*Bhel poori*)

SERVES 4–6

700 g/1½ lb puffed rice
1 medium potato, boiled and diced
    into 5 mm/¼ in cubes
1 small onion, finely chopped
2 tbsp coriander leaves, chopped
½ tsp salt

Tamarind chutney
about 120 ml/4 fl oz thick tamarind
    juice
½ tsp salt
½ tsp chilli powder
1½ tsp sugar

Green chutney
4 sprigs of coriander, washed
2 green chillies
½ tsp salt
2–3 tbsp lemon juice
a little water

1 Mix together the puffed rice, potato, onion, coriander leaves and salt and put aside.

2 Make the tamarind chutney by mixing together the tamarind juice, salt, chilli powder and sugar; put aside.

3 Make the green chutney by first chopping the coriander leaves and throwing away the lower stalks and roots.

4 Blend together the coriander leaves, green chillies, salt and lemon juice until smooth. Add a little water if necessary. This sauce should not be too thick.

5 When you are ready to serve bhel poori, add the chutneys to the puffed rice mixture (the amount can vary to suit individual taste). Serve immediately as a snack.

Opposite Savoury puffed rice/
Bhel poori

Rice with Gram Flour Dumplings
(*Gatte ki khichiri*)

SERVES 4

75 g/3 oz gram (chick pea) flour

¼ tsp chilli powder

½ tsp ground coriander

pinch of turmeric

½ tsp salt

2 tbsp hot, melted ghee (see
   page 21)

about 4 tbsp hot water

Rice

275 g/10 oz basmati rice

2 tbsp ghee

1 tsp cumin seeds

½ tsp chilli powder

900 ml/1½ pt boiling water

1 Sieve the gram flour into a large bowl.

2 Mix in the chilli powder, coriander, turmeric and half the salt. Rub in the ghee.

3 Add enough water to make a firm dough and knead for 2–3 minutes.

4 Divide into 4 parts. Roll each ball between your palms into round strips 15 cm/6 in long.

5 Bring some water to the boil and place these strips carefully in the water. Boil for 5 minutes. Drain and cool, then cut into 1 cm/½ in pieces.

6 Wash the basmati rice in several changes of water. Leave the rice to soak for 20 minutes in plenty of water and then drain.

7 In a large saucepan, heat the ghee over a medium high heat. Add the cumin seeds and let them sizzle for 3–4 seconds.

8 Add the rice, chilli powder and remaining salt, and sauté for 2–3 minutes.

9 Add the gram flour pieces carefully and gently mix with the rice. Fry for 1 minute.

10 Add the water and, when it starts to boil rapidly, lower the heat to very low, cover and cook for about 20 minutes until the rice is tender.

11 Fluff with a fork and serve hot.

Curry with Gram Flour Dumplings
(*Gatte ki saag*)

SERVES 4

Dough

75 g/3 oz gram (chick pea) flour
¼ tsp chilli powder
½ tsp ground coriander
good pinch of turmeric
¾ tsp salt
2 tbsp melted ghee (see page 21)
about 4 tbsp water

Curry

2 tbsp melted ghee (see page 21)
½ tsp cumin seeds
¼ tsp mustard seeds
pinch of asafoetida
120 ml/4 fl oz yoghurt, beaten well
½ tsp chilli powder
3 tsp ground coriander
½ tsp ground turmeric
I tsp salt

1 To make the dough, place the gram flour, chilli powder, coriander, turmeric and salt in a bowl. Rub in the ghee.

2 Add enough water to make a firm dough. Knead for 2–3 minutes.

3 Divide into 4 parts. Roll each ball between your palms into round strips 15 cm/6 in long.

4 Bring some water to the boil, and place the strips into the water carefully. Boil for 5 minutes. Drain and cool. Cut into 1 cm/½ in pieces.

5 To make the curry, heat the ghee in a saucepan over a medium heat. Add the cumin seeds, mustard and

asafoetida and let them splutter for 5–6 seconds.

6 Remove from the heat and add the yoghurt and the rest of the spices.

7 Stirring constantly, return the pan to the heat and cook for about 3–4 minutes (if you do not stir constantly the yoghurt might separate).

8 Add the gram flour pieces, mix gently with the gravy and cook for a further 5 minutes.

Fried Lentil Cakes
(*Vada*)

SERVES 4

225 g/8 oz channa dal, washed
I–2 green chillies, chopped
I small onion, finely chopped
pinch of asafoetida
½ tsp chilli powder (optional)
½ tsp salt
oil for deep frying

1 Soak the dal in plenty of cold water for 4–5 hours. Drain.

2 Grind the dal coarsely in a food processor or blender. (If using a blender, add a little water only if necessary.)

3 Add the green chillies, onions, asafoetida, chilli powder and salt to the ground dal and mix well.

4 Heat the oil over a medium high heat.

5 Take a tablespoon of the mixture in the palm of your hand, flatten it slightly and deep fry for 1–2 minutes until golden brown. Serve hot.

Opposite Rice with gram flour dumplings/Gatte ki khichiri

Below Fried Lentil Cakes/Vada

Spicy Ground Lamb Wrapped with Potatoes
(*Chop*)

SERVES 4

Filling

2 tbsp oil

1 large onion, finely sliced

2 cloves garlic, crushed

1 cm/½ in ginger, grated

¾ tsp ground turmeric

½ tsp chilli powder

1 tsp salt

good pinch of sugar

1 tbsp raisins (optional)

2 tsp vinegar

450 g/1 lb minced lamb

1 tsp ground garam masala

1 egg (slightly beaten)

breadcrumbs

oil for shallow frying

Chop

750 g/1¾ lb potatoes, peeled and boiled

1 tsp ground roasted cumin

½ tsp ground, roasted, dried red chillies (optional)

1 tsp salt

1 To make the filling, heat the oil in a large frying pan over a medium high heat. Add the onion, garlic and ginger and fry for 4–5 minutes, stirring constantly, until the onion becomes pale gold.

2 Add the turmeric, chilli, salt, sugar, raisins and vinegar, mix thoroughly with the onion and fry for 1 minute. Add the lamb and mix with the spices.

3 Cover, lower the heat, and, stirring occasionally, cook for about 20 minutes. Remove the cover, turn the heat up and, stirring constantly, cook until all the liquid has evaporated and the lamb is dry.

4 Mix in the garam masala, remove from the heat and set aside to cool.

5 To make the filling, mash the potatoes with the cumin, chilli and salt. Divide into 20–22 balls.

6 Take a ball and make a depression in the middle with your thumb, to form a cup shape. Fill the centre with the meat and re-form the potato ball, making sure no cracks appear. Make all the chop in this manner. (The chop can be round and flat or long in shape.)

Above Spicy ground lamb wrapped with potatoes/Chop

7 Place the chop in the egg, one at a time, and roll in the breadcrumbs.

8 Heat the oil over a very high heat in a large frying pan and fry the chop until golden brown, turning once (about 1 minute).

172

Fried potatoes
(*Aloo bhaja*)

SERVES 2
3–4 medium potatoes, peeled
½ tsp salt
oil for shallow frying

1 Slice the potatoes thinly and rub in the salt.

2 Heat the oil over a high heat and fry the potatoes until golden.

Fried Fish
(*Mach bhaja*)

SERVES 2
450 g/1 lb medium size herring,
    cleaned and washed
1 tsp salt
½ tsp ground turmeric
oil for shallow frying

1 Rub the salt and turmeric into the fish and leave aside for 15–20 minutes.

2 Heat the oil over a medium high heat and fry the fish for about 3–4 minutes on each side.

Fried Aubergine
(*Baigun bhaja*)

SERVES 2
1 large aubergine
½ tsp salt
pinch of ground turmeric
pinch of sugar
oil for shallow frying

1 Slice the aubergine into 1 cm/ ½ in thick rounds. Rub with the salt, turmeric and sugar and leave in a sieve for 30 minutes for the excess water to drain out.

2 Heat the oil over a medium high heat and fry the aubergine until brown in colour, turning once.

173

Vegetable Cutlet
(*Sabzi cutlet*)

SERVES 4
100 g/4 oz beetroot, diced
100 g/4 oz carrots, diced
225 g/8 oz potatoes, diced
100 g/4 oz cabbage, shredded
½ tsp chilli powder
½ tsp ground roasted cumin (see
    page 23)
½ tsp ground black pepper
¾ tsp salt
a big pinch of sugar
1 tbsp raisins (optional)
50 g/2 oz flour
120 ml/4 fl oz milk
breadcrumbs
oil for deep frying

1 Boil the beetroot, carrots, potatoes and cabbage together until
tender. Drain.

2 Mash the boiled vegetables with
the chilli, roasted cumin, black
pepper, salt, sugar and raisins.
Divide into 12 balls and flatten.
Chill for 1 hour.

3 Make a batter with the flour and
milk and dip a cutlet in it. Then
roll it in breadcrumbs until well
coated.

4 Heat the oil in a large frying pan
and fry the cutlets for 2–3 minutes
turning once, until crisp and golden.
Serve with Green coriander chutney
(see page 200).

Plantain Balls
(*Kela kofta*)

SERVES 2
1 plantain, cut in half
1 green chilli, chopped
½ tbsp chopped coriander leaves
½ tsp salt
1 tbsp onion, chopped
1 tsp plain flour
oil for deep frying

1 Boil the plantain until soft. Peel
and cool.

2 Mash the plantain with the
chilli, coriander leaves, salt, onion
and flour. Divide the mixture into 8
small balls and flatten.

3 Heat the oil and fry the koftas,
turning once, until crisp and golden.

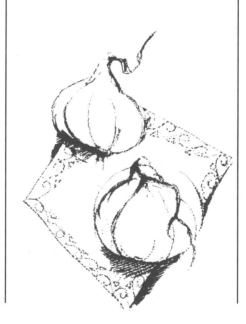

Right Plantain balls/Kela kofta

Fried Potato Cakes
(Aloo tikka)

SERVES 4
450 g/1 lb potatoes, boiled and
   mashed
1–2 green chillies, chopped
½ tsp salt
1 tbsp coriander leaves, chopped
2 tbsp onions, chopped
oil for frying

1 Mix the mashed potatoes with
the chillies, salt, coriander leaves
and onions.

2 Form into small balls and flatten.

3 Heat the oil until hot and fry the
potato cakes for a few minutes each
side until golden. Serve with a
chutney.

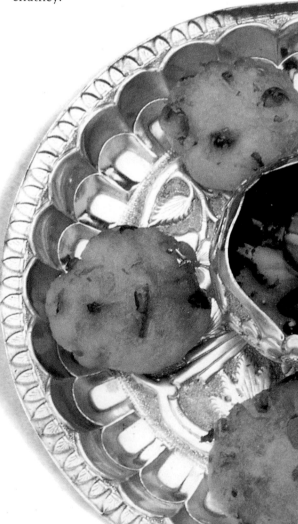

Lentil Cakes in Yoghurt
(Dahi vada)

SERVES 4
225 g/8 oz washed urid dal
450 ml/¾ pt water
3 green chillies
½ tsp salt
¼ tsp asafoetida
oil for deep frying
900 ml/1½ pt plain yoghurt
1 tsp ground roasted cumin (see
   page 23)
¼ tsp garam masala (see page 13)
½ tsp chilli powder

1 Wash the dal and soak in the
water overnight.

2 Put the dal, green chillies, salt
and asafoetida and some of the
soaking liquid in a liquidizer or a
food processor. Blend until you have
a thick paste, adding more soaking
liquid as necessary.

3 Heat the oil over medium high
heat in a karai.

4 Add tablespoons of the mixture
to the hot oil and fry for 3–4 minutes
until they are reddish brown, turning
once. Drain them on paper towels.

5 When all the vadas are fried put
them in a bowl of warm water for 1
minute. Squeeze out the water
gently and put in a large dish.

6 Combine the yoghurt, roasted
cumin, garam masala and chilli
powder and pour over the vadas.

7 Chill and serve with Tamarind
chutney (see page 198).

Rice and Lentil Pancake with a Potato Stuffing
(*Masala dosa*)

SERVES 4

200 g/7 oz rice, washed
65 g/2½ oz urid dal, washed
1 tsp salt
about 175 ml/6 fl oz water
a little oil for frying

Filling

4 tbsp oil
½ tsp mustard seeds
1 tbsp channa dal
⅓ tsp asafoetida
2 tbsp cashew nuts, chopped
   (optional)
8–10 curry leaves
2 cm/¾ in ginger, grated
3–4 green chillies, chopped

1 large onion, finely sliced
450 g/1 lb potatoes, peeled and
   diced into 5 mm/¼ in cubes and
   then boiled
½ tsp ground turmeric
1 tsp salt
120 ml/4 fl oz water

1 Soak the rice and urid dal separately in plenty of water and put aside for 6–8 hours. Drain.

2 In a liquidizer or food processor, blend the rice and dal separately to a fine paste. During the blending add a little water, if required.

3 Mix the two pastes together, add the salt and beat for 1–2 minutes.

4 Cover and keep aside in a warm place overnight to let it ferment.

5 Next morning, give the mixture a good stir and add enough water to make a thin pouring consistency.

6 To make the filling, heat 4 tbsp oil in a saucepan over a medium high heat, add the mustard seeds, channa dal, asafoetida, cashew nuts, curry leaves, ginger and green chillies and let them sizzle for 6–8 seconds.

7 Add the onion and fry until transparent.

8 Add the potatoes, turmeric and salt and mix with the other spices. Add the water, bring to the boil, cover and simmer over a medium heat for about 10 minutes until well mixed and all the water has evaporated. Put aside.

Above Rice and lentil pancake with a potato stuffing/Masala dhosa

9 To make the pancakes, heat a non-stick frying pan over a medium heat and brush with a little oil. Pour in a ladleful of the mixture and spread it like a pancake. Put a little more oil around the edges and a little on top. Cook for a couple of minutes until lightly golden. Turn the dosa and cook for a further couple of minutes.

10 Put on a plate, place a heaped tbsp of the hot filling on one end of the dosa, fold in half and serve hot with Coconut chutney (see page 196) and Lentils with vegetables II (see page 32). (It can also be folded to make a triangle.)

Opposite above Lentil cakes in yoghurt/Dahi vada

Left Fried potato cakes/Aloo tikka

177

Savoury Semolina
(*Uppuma*)

SERVES 4
175 g/6 oz coarse semolina
2 tbsp unsalted peanuts, chopped
3 tbsp oil
¼ tsp mustard seeds
2 tsp urid dal
1 tsp channa dal
1 medium onion, finely chopped
10–12 curry leaves
1 small carrot, cut into thin strips
　　about 5 cm/2 in long
2 tbsp peas
4–5 French beans, cut into thin strips
　　about 5 cm/2 in long
1 tsp salt
about 750 ml/1¼ pt water
juice of ½ a lemon

1 Dry roast the semolina until lightly golden. Put aside.

2 Dry roast the peanuts until golden and put aside.

3 Heat the oil over a medium heat, add the mustard seeds, urid and channa dals and when they stop spluttering, add the onion and 8 of the curry leaves. Fry until the onion is golden in colour.

4 Add the vegetables and stir fry for 2–3 minutes.

5 Add the semolina and mix with the other ingredients and continue to fry for a further 1–2 minutes.

6 Add the salt and water and, stirring constantly, cook until all the water evaporates and the mixture is absolutely dry.

7 Squeeze on the lemon juice and mix in the remaining curry leaves.

8 Garnish with the roasted peanuts. Serve hot with Coconut chutney (see page 196) as a light meal.

Vegetable Fritters
(*Pakoras*)

SERVES 4
Batter
4 tbsp gram (chick pea) flour
2 tsp oil
1 tsp baking powder
½ tsp salt
85 ml/3 fl oz water
**Any of the following vegetables can
　be used**
aubergines, cut into very thin rounds
onions, cut into 2 mm/⅛ in rings
potatoes, cut into very thin rounds

cauliflower, cut into 2 cm/¾ in
    florets
chilli, left whole
pumpkin, cut into thin slices
green pepper, cut into thin strips
oil for deep frying

1 Mix all the batter ingredients together and beat until smooth.

2 Wash the slices of vegetables and pat dry.

3 Heat the oil in a karai until it is very hot.

4 Dip a slice of the vegetable in the batter and put into the hot oil. Place as many slices as you can in the oil. Fry until crisp and golden. Drain and serve with either Mint or Green coriander chutney (see page 200).

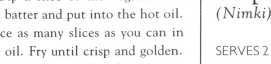

Deep Fried Pastry
(*Nimki*)

SERVES 2
100 g/4 oz flour
½ tsp salt
pinch of kalonji
pinch of ground roasted cumin (see page 23)
1½ tbsp oil
approx. 50 ml/2 fl oz hot water
oil for deep frying

1 Sieve the flour and salt together. Mix in the kalonji and cumin. Rub in the 1½ tbsp oil.

2 Add enough water to make a stiff dough. Knead for 10 minutes until soft and smooth.

3 Divide the dough into 12 balls. Roll each ball into thin rounds 10 cm/4 in across. Make 5 or 6 small cuts in the rounds.

4 Heat the oil in a karai over medium heat. Add a nimki and fry until crisp and golden. Drain on paper towels. Serve with chutney or Dry potatoes (see page 80).

Left Vegetable fritters/Pakoras

Savoury Potato Snack
(*Aloo kabli*)

SERVES 2

350 g/12 oz potatoes, boiled and
    peeled
1 small onion, finely chopped
1–2 green chillies, finely chopped
½ tsp salt
½ tsp chilli powder
5–6 tbsp tamarind juice (see
    page 22)
1 tbsp coriander leaves, chopped

1 Cut the potatoes into 5mm/¼ in slices and cool thoroughly.

2 Gently mix in all the other ingredients. Serve cold.

Below Savoury potato snack/
Aloo kabli

Cheese Cutlet
(*Panir cutlet*)

SERVES 4

1 tbsp ghee (see page 21)
250 ml/8 fl oz milk
175 g/6 oz panir (see page 20),
    drained
100 g/4 oz semolina
1 medium onion, finely chopped
2 green chillies, finely chopped
1 tbsp coriander leaves, chopped
½ tsp salt
2 tbsp flour
120 ml/4 fl oz milk
breadcrumbs
oil for deep frying

1 Heat the ghee in a karai over medium heat, add the milk, panir, semolina, onions, chilli, coriander leaves and salt and mix thoroughly. Stirring constantly, cook until the mixture leaves the sides and a ball forms, about 3–4 minutes.

2 Spread the mixture 2 cm/¾ in thick on a greased baking tin. Cut into 2.5 cm/1 in squares and chill for about 2 hours.

3 Make a smooth batter with the flour and milk. Dip each square in the batter and then roll it in breadcrumbs.

Above Cheese cutlet/Panir cutlet

4 Heat the oil in a karai over high heat and fry the cutlets for 2–3 minutes till crisp and golden. Serve with chutney.

181

Wholewheat Pastry with Potato Stuffing
(*Bhakhar vadi*)

SERVES 4

700 g/1½ lb potatoes, washed and peeled
2 green chillies
1 cm/½ in ginger
3 tbsp oil
½ tsp mustard seeds
pinch of asafoetida
2 dried red chillies
¼ tsp chilli powder
pinch of ground turmeric
2 tsp salt
1½ tsp mango powder
½ tsp sugar
225 g/8 oz wholewheat flour
100 g/4 oz plain flour
about 5 tbsp warm water
oil for deep frying

1 Finely grate the potatoes and soak in water for about 30 minutes. Drain and dry thoroughly.

2 Grind the green chillies and ginger to a paste.

3 Heat 2 tbsp of the oil over a medium high heat. Add the mustard, asafoetida and red chillies and let them sizzle for 8–10 seconds.

4 Add the dried potatoes, chilli powder, turmeric, 1 tsp salt and the chilli and ginger paste and stir fry for 5–7 minutes.

5 Lower the heat slightly, cover and, stirring occasionally, cook for about 25–30 minutes until the potatoes are tender. Add the mango powder and sugar, and mix. Remove from the heat, cool and divide into 4 parts.

6 Sieve together the wholewheat flour, plain flour and 1 tsp salt. Rub in 1 tbsp of oil.

7 Add enough water to make a stiff dough. Knead for 7–10 minutes to make the dough soft and pliable. Divide into 4 portions.

8 Take a portion and roll into a 20 cm/8 in round on a lightly floured surface. Spread a portion of the potato mixture evenly on the rolled dough. Starting at the side closest to you, carefully roll it up tightly like a jelly roll. Cut into slices 1 cm/½ in thick. Gently flatten each slice between the palms of your hands.

9 Heat the oil for deep frying and carefully fry them for 3–4 minutes until they are golden; turn once. These can be eaten as a snack or as an accompaniment to a main meal.

Steamed Lentil Cakes
(*Dhokla*)

SERVES 4

225 g/8 oz channa dal
4 tbsp water
3 green chillies
1 cm/ ½ in ginger
1 tsp salt
pinch of turmeric
¾ tsp baking soda
juice of 1 lime
1 tbsp oil
½ tsp mustard seeds
pinch of asafoetida
1 tbsp coconut, grated
1 tbsp coriander leaves, chopped

1 Soak the channa dal overnight in plenty of cold water. The next morning, wash the dal 2 or 3 times.

2 Place the dal and the water in a food processor or blender and blend until smooth.

3 Grind the chillies and ginger together to a paste.

4 Add the chilli and ginger paste, salt, turmeric, baking soda and lime juice to the blended dal and mix thoroughly.

5 Pour the mixture into a greased thali or a shallow cake pan, making sure that it does not come more than three quarters of the way up.

6 Place the thali in a steamer, cover and steam for 20 minutes. Remove from the heat and set aside for 5 minutes. Insert a skewer into the middle to test whether the dhoklas are cooked.

7 Cut into 4 cm/1½ in squares and arrange on a plate.

8 Heat the oil in a small saucepan and add the mustard seeds; when they start to splutter, add the asafoetida and, after 2–3 seconds, pour this over the dhoklas.

9 Garnish with the coconut and coriander leaves.

Opposite Steamed lentil cakes/ Dhokla

Rolled Gram Flour Paste
(Khandvi)

SERVES 4

175 g/6 oz gram (chick pea) flour
4 tbsp yoghurt
350 ml/12 fl oz water
2 green chillies
1 cm/½ in ginger
pinch of ground turmeric
¾ tsp salt
1 tbsp oil
½ tsp mustard seeds
pinch of asafoetida
2 tbsp coconut, grated
2 tbsp coriander leaves, chopped

1 Sieve the gram flour into a large bowl.

2 Lightly beat the yoghurt and water together.

3 Grind the chillies and ginger together to make a paste.

4 Add the yoghurt and water mixture and the paste to the gram flour and whisk until smooth. Stir in the turmeric and salt. Put the mixture to one side for 1 hour.

5 Pour the mixture into a saucepan and heat gently, stirring constantly until it thickens. (Be careful to let no lumps form).

6 When the mixture thickens, spread a little thinly on a greased plate and let it cool. Try to roll it; if you cannot, thicken the mixture a little more.

Above Rolled gram flour paste/
Khandvi

7 Grease 2 or 3 large plates and spread the mixture very thinly on them with the back of a spatula. Allow the mixture to cool.

8 Cut into strips 5 mm/¼ in long, and, starting at one end of each strip, roll them up. Place these rolls in a flat serving dish, one next to the other.

9 Heat the oil until very hot. Add the mustard seeds and asafoetida and let them sizzle for 8–10 seconds. Pour this over the rolled khandvi and garnish with the coconut and coriander leaves.

Fried Lentil Balls
(Dal vada)

SERVES 4

225 g/8 oz urid dal, washed
5–6 curry leaves
2–3 green chillies
pinch of asafoetida
1 cm/½ in ginger, grated
¾ tsp cumin seeds
1 tsp salt
oil for deep frying

1 Soak the urid dal in plenty of cold water overnight. Drain.

2 In a liquidizer or food processor, blend the dal with all the other ingredients. Add a little water, if necessary, to make a fine, thick paste.

3 Heat the oil over a medium high heat. Drop in a teaspoonful of the mixture and fry until nicely golden. Serve with a chutney as a snack or as an accompaniment to a main meal.

Yoghurt Curry
(*Karhi*)

SERVES 2
Pakoras
75 g/3 oz gram (chick pea) flour
¼ tsp salt
pinch of ground turmeric
about 4 tbsp water
oil for deep frying
Curry
300 ml/½ pt yoghurt
350 ml/12 fl oz water
1 tbsp gram (chick pea) flour
1 tbsp oil
¼ tsp fenugreek seeds
pinch of asafoetida
6–8 curry leaves
2 green chillies, chopped
½ tsp ground turmeric
½ tsp chilli powder
½ tsp salt

1 To make the pakoras, make a thick batter with the gram flour, salt, turmeric and water.

2 Heat the oil over a medium high heat, drop in a teaspoonful of the batter and fry until crisp and golden. Drain and set aside.

3 To make the curry, whisk the yoghurt, water and gram flour until smooth.

4 Place the fried pakoras in a bowl of water for 3–4 minutes. Gently squeeze out as much water as possible and put aside.

5 Heat 1 tbsp oil in a large saucepan over a medium heat. Add the fenugreek, asafoetida, curry leaves and green chillies and let them sizzle for about 10 seconds.

6 Add the yoghurt mixture, turmeric, chilli and salt and slowly bring to a boil.

7 Lower the heat, add the pakoras and simmer for about 10 minutes until the sauce has thickened. Serve hot with rice.

Below Yoghurt curry/Karhi

Samosas

SERVES 4

Filling

3 tbsp oil

¼ tsp whole cumin seeds

450 g/1 lb potatoes, diced into
    1 cm/½ in cubes

1 green chilli, finely chopped

pinch of turmeric

½ tsp salt

75 g/3 oz peas

1 tsp ground roasted cumin (see
    page 23)

Dough

225 g/8 oz plain flour

1 tsp salt

3 tbsp oil

approx. 100 ml/3 ½ fl oz hot water

oil for deep frying

1 To make the filling, heat the oil in a karai over medium high heat and add the cumin seeds. Let them sizzle for a few seconds.

2 Add the potatoes and green chilli and fry for 2–3 minutes. Add the turmeric and salt and, stirring occasionally, cook for 5 minutes.

3 Add the peas and the ground roasted cumin. Stir to mix. Cover, lower the heat and cook a further 10 minutes until the potatoes are tender. Cool.

4 To make the dough, sieve together the flour and salt. Rub in the oil. Add enough water to form a stiff dough. Knead for 10 minutes until smooth.

5 Divide into 12 balls. Roll each ball into a round of about 15 cm/ 6 in across. Cut in half.

6 Pick up one half, flatten it slightly and form a cone, sealing the overlapping edge with a little

water. Fill the cone with 1½ tsp of the filling and seal the top with a little water.

7 Make all the samosas in the same way.

8 Heat the oil in a karai over medium heat. Put as many samosas as you can into the hot oil and fry until crisp and golden. Drain. Serve with a chutney.

Cabbage Salad
(*Kacha pakka kobi*)

SERVES 4

450 g/1 lb green cabbage
1 tsp oil
2 green chillies, chopped
2 tsp urid dal
½ tsp mustard seeds
pinch of asafoetida
¾ tsp coconut, grated
1 tbsp coriander leaves, chopped

1 Cut the cabbage very finely into long strips. Wash and dry them.

2 Heat the oil in a large saucepan over a medium high heat. Add the chillies and fry for 3–4 seconds.

3 Remove the pan from the heat, add the urid dal and stir fry until lightly golden (this will take a few seconds only).

4 Put the pan back on the heat and add the mustard seeds; after 8–10 seconds add the asafoetida and fry for 2–3 seconds.

5 Add the cabbage and salt and, stirring constantly, cook for 3–4 minutes. Serve garnished with the coconut and coriander leaves.

Cucumber Salad
(*Khamang kakadi*)

SERVES 4

2 tbsp unsalted peanuts
½ cucumber, peeled and cut into
    fine strips
2 tbsp grated coconut
2 tbsp lemon juice
½ tsp salt
1 tbsp melted ghee (see page 21)
¼ tsp cumin seeds
pinch of asafoetida
2 green chillies, chopped
1 tbsp coriander leaves, chopped

1 Dry roast the peanuts and grind them to a fine powder.

2 Gently squeeze the cucumber to get rid of the excess water.

Above Cucumber salad/
Khamang kakadi

3 Place the cucumber, coconut, ground peanuts, lemon juice and salt in a bowl and mix gently.

4 In a small saucepan, heat the ghee. Add the cumin seeds and let them sizzle for 3–4 seconds. Add the asafoetida and the green chillies and fry for 5–6 seconds. Pour this over the cucumber mixture and mix well.

5 Garnish with the coriander leaves.

Spicy Sago
(*Saboodana ki khichiri*)

SERVES 4
175 g/6 oz sago
75 g/3 oz peanuts, skinned
2 tbsp oil
1 tsp mustard seeds
2 green chillies, chopped
pinch of asafoetida
good pinch of turmeric
1 tsp salt
1 tsp sugar
about 5 tbsp water
juice of ½ a lime
1 tbsp coconut, grated
1 tbsp coriander leaves, chopped

1 Wash the sago and soak in a little water for about 10 minutes. Drain and dry on paper towelling.

2 Roast the peanuts and grind coarsely.

3 Mix the sago and peanuts.

4 Heat the oil in a saucepan over a medium high heat. Add the mustard seeds and green chillies; when the mustard seeds start to splutter, add the asafoetida and fry for 2–3 seconds.

5 Add the sago and peanut mixture, turmeric, salt and sugar and stir fry for 1 minute.

6 Lower the heat and continue to stir fry for another 2–3 minutes.

7 Add the water, cover and cook, stirring occasionally, until the sago is tender and nearly dry.

8 Add the lime juice and give it a good stir. Serve garnished with coconut and coriander leaves.

Below Spicy sago/Saboodana ki khichiri

Melon with Orange Juice

(Tarbuch aur mosamki ka rus)

SERVES 4

1 honeydew melon
15 g/½ oz butter or ghee
½ tsp ground cumin
juice of 2 sweet oranges
1 tbsp lemon juice
2 tbsp sugar

1 Cut the melon into segments, remove the pith and seeds and cut the flesh from the skin. Cut into cubes.

2 Heat the butter or ghee in a pan, add the cumin and let it sizzle until the fragrance emerges.

3 Meanwhile, mix the orange and lemon juice with the sugar and 1 tbsp water.

4 Sprinkle the syrup on the melon, add the cumin and serve.

Tomato Salad
(Kachumbar)

Above Tomato salad/Kachumbar

SERVES 4

450 g/1 lb tomatoes, sliced
2 green chillies, finely sliced
2 tsp sugar
1 tbsp lemon juice
leaves from 1 or 2 sprigs of
    coriander
salt

1 Mix the tomato with the chilli.

2 Sprinkle with sugar, lemon juice and coriander leaves. Mix well and add salt to taste.

Right Melon with orange juice/
Tarbuh aur moramki ka rus

Chicken and Vegetable Salad
(Murghi aur kachumbar)

SERVES 4–6
225 g/8 oz cooked chicken, cut into
   manageable pieces
1 or 2 apples, cored and cut into
   segments
75 g/3 oz white cabbage, shredded
2 tomatoes, cut into 8
1 green chilli, finely chopped
½ tsp ground pepper
¼ tsp ground nutmeg
salt
2 tbsp lemon juice
leaves from 1 or 2 sprigs coriander

1 Mix the chicken with the apple, cabbage, tomato and green chilli.

2 Sprinkle on the pepper, nutmeg and salt.

3 Squeeze over the lemon juice and toss the salad. Decorate with coriander leaves.

Above Chicken and vegetable salad/
Murghi aur kachumbar

Below Cabbage fritters/
Gobi pakoras

Cabbage Fritters
(Gobi pakoras)

SERVES 4
100 g/4 oz gram flour (besan)
100 g/4 oz hard white cabbage,
   grated
1 small onion, finely sliced
2 green chillies, thinly sliced
15 g/½ oz fresh ginger, finely grated
4–6 curry leaves, chopped
1 tsp salt
½ tsp chilli powder
½ tsp garam masala (see page 13)
oil for deep frying

1 Mix the flour with 150 ml/¼ pt water to make a batter.

2 Add all the ingredients except the oil and stir well to coat.

3 Heat a quantity of oil for deep frying, add the cabbage in batter by the tablespoonful and fry until golden. Drain on absorbent kitchen paper.

4 Serve with chutney.

Chutneys, Pickles and Relishes

· ·

Pickles and chutneys can be spicy, sweet, tart, hot, sour, mild or aromatic. The more variety, the better. They are best served with plain foods such as rice and bread, or with lightly spiced dishes. They should not have to compete with the flavour of the dish they accompany, and they should certainly not overwhelm it.

A yoghurt relish called raita is often served to provide a cooling contrast to a hot spicy meal.

Yoghurt with Cucumber
(*Kheera raita*)

325 ml/12 fl oz unsweetened yoghurt
1–2 green chillies, chopped
2 tbsp chopped coriander leaves
½ cucumber, finely sliced
½ tsp chilli powder
½ tsp ground roasted cumin (see
   page 23)
½ tsp salt

1 Place the yoghurt in a bowl and whisk until smooth.

2 Add all the other ingredients and stir in well. Chill.

Above Yoghurt with cucumber/
Kheera raita

Below Yoghurt with boondi/
Boondi raita

Yoghurt with Boondi
(*Boondi raita*)

75 g/3 oz boondi
325 ml/12 fl oz unsweetened yoghurt
½ tsp salt
½ tsp chilli powder
pinch of paprika
pinch of garam masala (see page 13)

1 Soak the boondi in a little cold water for 10–15 minutes.

2 Beat the yoghurt in a bowl until smooth. Add the salt and chilli powder and stir.

3 Gently squeeze the boondi to remove the water and add to the spiced yoghurt. Mix well and chill. Before serving sprinkle with paprika and garam masala.

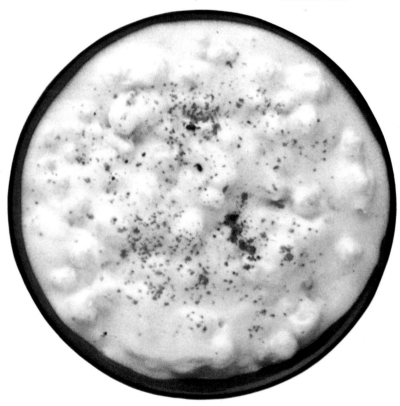

Yoghurt with Potatoes
(Aloo raita)

450 ml/16 fl oz unsweetened yoghurt
275 g/10 oz potatoes, boiled and
    diced into 5 mm/¼ in cubes
1 small onion, finely chopped
½ tsp salt
¼ tsp ground black pepper
½ tsp ground roasted cumin (see
    page 23)
1 green chilli, chopped
1 tbsp coriander leaves

1 Beat the yoghurt in a bowl until smooth.

2 Add the potatoes, onions, salt, pepper and cumin and gently mix. Chill.

3 Serve sprinkled with the chilli and coriander leaves.

Above Yoghurt with potatoes/
Aloo raita

Below Yoghurt with aubergine/
Baigan raita

Yoghurt with Aubergine
(Baigan raita)

6–8 tbsp oil
1 small aubergine, cut into small
    pieces
325 ml/12 fl oz unsweetened yoghurt
½ tsp salt
½ tsp ground roasted cumin (see
    page 23)
½ tsp chilli powder

1 Heat the oil in a karai and fry the aubergine pieces until brown. Drain.

2 Place the yoghurt in a bowl and whisk until smooth. Add the salt, cumin and chilli and mix thoroughly.

3 Place the fried aubergine pieces in a bowl and pour over the spiced yoghurt. Chill.

195

Yoghurt and Tomato Relish
(Tamatar raita)

100 g/4 oz tomatoes, diced
I small onion, finely chopped
150 ml/¼ pt yoghurt
leaves from I sprig of coriander
I green chilli, finely chopped
15 g/½ oz fresh ginger, finely grated
½ tsp salt
½ tsp ground cumin, roasted
   without fat

1 Mix the tomato with the onion. You can reduce the strength of the onion by rinsing it in hot water, if preferred.

2 Mix the yoghurt with the remaining ingredients. Stir the dressing into the vegetables and add extra salt to taste.

Coconut Chutney
(Thankai chatni)

100 g/4 oz finely grated coconut
3 red chillies, chopped and seeded
50 ml/2 fl oz yoghurt
I tbsp oil
½ tsp mustard seeds
4 curry leaves
salt

1 Grind, pound or blend in a liquidizer the coconut and 2 red chillies, then stir in the yoghurt.

2 Heat the oil, add the mustard seeds and fry until they have all popped, then add the remaining red chilli and the curry leaves and continue to fry for 2–3 minutes.

3 Add to the coconut mix with salt to taste.

(Photograph, see page 192)

Below Yoghurt and tomato relish/
Tamatar raita

Above Mango pickle/Aam ki aachar

Mango Pickle
(*Aam ki aachar*)

10 green mangoes
½ tsp fenugreek seeds, ground
6 tbsp ground mustard
3 tsp salt
450 ml/16 fl oz mustard oil
1 tsp asafoetida
juice of 1 lime

1 Wash the mangoes and pat dry. Cut into 4 pieces, lengthwise. (Do not peel.)

2 Add the fenugreek, mustard and salt to the mangoes and mix well. Put aside for 15 minutes.

3 Heat the oil in a karai or saucepan over a medium heat. Add the asafoetida and let it sizzle for 5–6 seconds.

4 Add the mangoes, and, stirring occasionally, fry until the mangoes are tender and well mixed.

5 Remove from the heat and, when it becomes lukewarm, stir in the lime juice.

Tamarind Chutney
(*Amli chatni*)

1 tbsp coriander seeds
1 tsp peppercorns
½ tsp cumin seeds
½ tsp fenugreek seeds
1 tsp mustard seeds
½ tsp asafoetida
5 red chillies
2–3 tbsp oil
1 tsp polished split black lentils (urid dal)
1 tsp channa dal soaked for 20 minutes, then drained
6 curry leaves
25 g/1 oz shelled peanuts
juice from 225 g/8 oz seedless tamarind (see page 22)
2 tbsp brown sugar
salt
1 tbsp sesame seeds
25–50 g/1–2 oz desiccated coconut

1 Heat a frying pan without any butter or oil and add the coriander, peppercorns, cumin, fenugreek, half the mustard seeds, half the asafoetida and 4 red chillies. Roast the spices for about 5 minutes, shaking the pan to prevent burning. Pound or grind the spices to a fine powder and set aside.

2 Heat the oil in a pan, add the remaining mustard seeds, lentils, channa dal, curry leaves and remaining chilli, cut into 3 or 4 pieces, and fry until all the seeds have popped.

3 Add the peanuts and fry for a further 3 or 4 minutes, then add the tamarind juice, the roasted spice powder, sugar, ½ tsp salt and remaining asafoetida.

4 Heat another pan without fat or oil, roast the sesame seeds and coconut and add to the chutney. Stir well, adding extra salt to taste.

Tomato, Onion and Cucumber Relish
(*Kachumbar*)

1 large cucumber, finely chopped
4 medium onions, finely chopped
2 large tomatoes, finely chopped
2 green chillies, finely chopped
5–6 chopped coriander leaves
2–3 tbsp lime juice
1 tsp salt

1 Mix all the ingredients together.

2 Chill for 2–3 hours before serving.

Left Tamarind chutney/Amli chatni

Peanut Soya Sauce
(*Seng dana chatni*)

100 g/4 oz shelled peanuts, skinned
2 red chillies, cut into 3 or 4 pieces
½ tsp salt
2 tbsp soya sauce
1 tbsp lemon juice
1 tbsp brown sugar
2 tbsp oil

1 Pound, grind or blend in a liquidizer the first 6 ingredients.

2 Heat the oil in a pan, add the peanut mix, cook until it begins to bubble, then take off the heat and stir well.

Sweet Tomato Chutney
(*Tamatar ki chatni*)

450 g/1 lb tomatoes
50 g/2 oz sugar
½ tsp ground cardamom seeds
3 cloves
½ tsp chilli powder
1 tbsp oil
½ tsp mustard seeds
1 tbsp white wine vinegar
salt
4 curry leaves

1 Immerse the tomatoes in a bowl of boiling water for about 2 minutes, until the skins split, drain them, allow to cool, peel and chop.

2 Bring 150 ml/¼ pt of water to the boil in a small pan, add the sugar and tomato and cook for 5 minutes, stirring.

3 Add the cardamom, cloves and chilli and continue cooking,

Above Sweet tomato chutney/
Tamata ki chatni

mashing the tomato under the back of a wooden spoon to make a thick paste. Remove the pan from the heat.

4 Heat the oil, add the mustard seeds and fry until they have all popped, then add to the tomato.

5 Stir in the vinegar, add salt to taste and sprinkle the curry leaves over the top.

Right Peanut soya sauce/
Seng dana chatni

199

Green Coriander Chutney
(*Hari daniya chatni*)

leaves from 3–4 sprigs coriander
1 or 2 green chillies
15 g/½ oz fresh ginger, grated
salt
2 tbsp lemon juice
½ tsp sugar

1 Grind, pound or blend in a liquidizer the coriander leaves, green chilli, ginger and ½ tsp salt to make a thick paste.

2 Stir in the lemon juice and add sugar and extra salt to taste.

Mint Chutney
(*Poodina ki chutney*)

handful mint leaves, washed
50 ml/2 fl oz tamarind juice
2 tbsp chopped onions
2 cloves garlic
2 cm/¾ in ginger
2–3 green chillies
½ tsp salt
½ tsp sugar

1 Blend all the ingredients together until you have a smooth paste.

Can be stored in an airtight container in the refrigerator for one week only.

Above Green coriander chutney/
Hari daniya chatni

Opposite Black lentil chutney/
Urid dal chatni

Black Lentil Curry
(Urid dal chatni)

75–100 g/3–4 oz polished split black
   lentils (urid dal)
1 or 2 red chillies
¼ tsp asafoetida
50 g/2 oz finely grated coconut
juice from 25 g/1 oz seedless
   tamarind (see page 22)
salt

1 Pick over the dal. Heat a pan without fat or oil, add the dal, 1 chilli and the asafoetida and cook, shaking the pan to prevent burning, until the dal is golden.

2 Pound the roasted spices together.

3 Grind, pound or blend in a liquidizer the coconut and tamarind with 1–2 tbsp water, then add the roasted spice powder and grind them together, adding a little more water if necessary.

4 Add salt to taste.

Green Mango Chutney
(Aam chatni)

225 g/8 oz hard green mango
50 g/2 oz finely grated coconut
1 red chilli or 1 tsp chilli powder
1 tsp mustard seeds
1 tbsp yoghurt
1 tbsp oil
4 curry leaves
salt

1 Chop the mango as finely as possible, with or without the skin.

2 Grind, pound or blend in a liquidizer the coconut, chilli and half the mustard seeds, add to the mango and stir in the yoghurt.

3 Heat the oil in a pan, add the remaining mustard seeds and the curry leaves and fry until all the seeds have popped, then stir into the chutney. Add salt to taste.

Below Green mango chutney/
Aam chatni

Desserts

. . . .

Indians look forward to their dessert and it is often the climax of the meal. Most sweets are milk-based and can be prepared in advance.

Ice Cream with Almonds and Pistachio Nuts
(*Kulfi*)

SERVES 6

1.2 litres/2 pt milk

50 g/2 oz sugar

2 tbsp ground almonds

2 tbsp pistachio nuts, skinned and
   chopped

few drops rose water

In India, kulfi is usually frozen in individual, conical shaped metal containers with lids. To break up the ice crystals during freezing, instead of stirring the mixture, the containers are gently rolled between the palms of your hands. To serve, they are once again rolled between the palms, removed from the containers and cut into thick slices.

Kulfi can be made easily in any kind of container that can be placed in the freezer.

1 Bring the milk to a boil, stirring constantly.

2 Lower the heat and simmer, stirring occasionally, until it reduces to about 500 ml/18 fl oz.

3 Add the sugar and mix thoroughly. Continue to simmer for another 2–3 minutes. Remove from the heat and let it cool completely.

4 Add the almonds and mix into the thickened milk, making sure no lumps form.

5 Stir in the pistachio nuts and rose water.

Mango Soufflé
(*Aam pudding*)

SERVES 4

4 eggs

2 tsp gelatine

300 ml/½ pt mango juice or 225 g/
   8oz mango pulp

2 tsp granulated sugar

salt

2 tbsp caster sugar

½ tsp vanilla flavouring

1 Separate the eggs, putting the yolks into a mixing bowl.

2 In a small bowl, mix the gelatine with 3 tbsp water.

3 Beat the yolks well and mix thoroughly with the mango juice or pulp.

4 Stir in the granulated sugar, gelatine and ½ tsp salt.

Above Mango soufflé/Aam pudding

5 Put the mixing bowl over a pan of boiling water, taking care that the bowl does not touch the water or the eggs will scramble. Beat the mixture for 10 minutes, then remove from the heat.

6 Whisk the egg whites with ½ tsp salt and the caster sugar until stiff, then fold into the yolks, adding the vanilla flavouring.

7 Divide the mixture between 4 small dishes and chill before serving.

6 Place the mixture in a dish, cover it with its own lid or aluminium foil and place it in the freezer.

7 Take it out of the freezer after 20 minutes and give it a good stir to break up the ice crystals. Repeat twice more.

8 After this, it may be divided up into six chilled individual dishes, and covered and frozen for about 4–5 hours. Take it out of the freezer about 10 minutes before you are ready to serve.

Below Pumpkin halva/Pethi halva

Pumpkin Halva
(Pethi halva)

SERVES 4
450 g/1 lb pumpkin (preferably white)
600 ml/1 pt milk
150 g/5 oz sugar
1 tsp rose water
100 g/4 oz ghee (see page 21)
¼ tsp ground cardamom seeds
10–15 cashew nuts, halved

1 Scrape the seeds and stringy bits from the inside of the pumpkin, cut the flesh from the skin and chop into chunks.

2 Grate the pumpkin coarsely, put in a muslin cloth and squeeze out all the moisture.

3 Put the pumpkin in a pan with the milk, sugar and rose water and cook over a low heat for 30 minutes or more, stirring briskly, until all the milk has evaporated.

4 Stir in the ghee and continue cooking until it separates. Drain off any butter not absorbed by the pumpkin mixture.

5 Stir in the cardamom and cashew nuts and spread the mixture in a greased dish with straight sides, in one layer about 5 cm/2 in deep.

6 Leave for about 45 minutes, until set, then cut into squares.

Beetroot Halva
(*Chukander halva*)

SERVES 4
450 g/1 lb beetroot
600 ml/1 pt milk
175 g/6 oz sugar
100 g/4 oz ghee (see page 21)
¼ tsp ground cardamom seeds
10 almonds

1 Scrape the skin from the beetroot, then grate coarsely.

2 Put the beetroot in a pan with the milk and sugar and cook gently for 30 minutes or more, stirring briskly, until all the milk has evaporated.

3 Add the ghee, cardamom and almonds and continue cooking, stirring all the time, until the mixture is heavy and sticky.

4 Spread the mixture in a greased dish with straight sides, in one layer about 5 cm/2 in deep.

5 Leave for about 45 minutes to set, then cut into squares.

South Indian Creamed Rice
(*Payasam*)

SERVES 4
90 g/3½ oz rice
1.2 litres/2 pt milk
75 g/3 oz jaggery (raw palm sugar) or brown sugar
1 tbsp cashew nuts, roasted

1 Wash the rice and set aside in a sieve to drain for 20 minutes.

2 Bring the milk to a boil in a large saucepan, stirring constantly.

3 Lower the heat, add the rice and stir well to mix.

4 Simmer until the rice is tender and the milk slightly thickened.

5 Add the jaggery or brown sugar, stir to mix and simmer for a further 5–7 minutes.

6 Stir in the cashew nuts and remove from the heat.

Pineapple Pudding
(*Ananas pudding*)

SERVES 2
225 g/8 oz canned pineapple chunks, drained
2 eggs
150 ml/¼ pt milk
100 g/4 oz sugar
¼ tsp ground cinnamon
3 cloves

1 Arrange the pineapple pieces in a greased ovenproof dish.

2 Beat the eggs with the milk and sugar and pour over the pineapple, then sprinkle on the cinnamon and cloves.

3 Set the dish in a roasting tray of boiling water and cook in the oven at 160°C/325°F/Gas 3 for about 45 minutes until lightly set.

Left Pineapple pudding/
Ananas pudding

Steamed Plantain Cake
(Kela cake)

SERVES 4

3 or 4 ripe plantain, peeled and thinly sliced
175–225 g/6–8 oz self-raising flour
1 tbsp melted ghee (see page 21)
50 g/2 oz finely grated coconut
175 g/6 oz brown sugar
½ tsp ground cardamom seeds

1 Sieve the flour into a bowl, make a well in the middle and pour in the melted ghee. Gradually adding as little warm water as possible (about 6 tbsp), work the ingredients into a smooth dough.

2 Mix the plantain with the remaining ingredients.

3 Cut kitchen foil into 4×23 cm/9 in squares and divide the dough between them. With your finger or a spoon, dipped in water to prevent sticking, spread the dough out to within 2.5 cm/1 in lengths of each side of the square.

4 Divide the plantain mix between the sheets of dough and spread to cover.

5 Fold each foil sheet over in the middle and fold over the edges, pressing down well to seal.

6 Put the foil parcels in a steamer over a pan of boiling water and steam, covered, for 25–30 minutes, making sure that the foil does not touch the water.

Creamed Rice
(Kheer)

SERVES 4
2 tbsp basmati rice
1.2 litres/2 pt milk
65 g/2½ oz sugar
2 tbsp peeled almonds
¼ tsp ground cardamom
I tsp rose water

1 Wash the rice in several changes of water and soak in plenty of water for 30 minutes. Drain.

2 Bring the milk to a boil over a high heat, stirring constantly. Lower the heat and simmer for 30 minutes, stirring occasionally.

3 Add the drained rice and sugar and continue to cook for a further 30–40 minutes until the milk has thickened and the rice is very soft and disintegrated.

4 Add the almonds and continue to cook for a further 10 minutes.

5 Remove from the heat and stir in the cardamom and rose water.

6 Place in a serving dish and refrigerate. Serve chilled.

Opposite Steamed plantain cake/
    Kela cake

Plantain Jaggery
(Kela gur)

SERVES 4
4 ripe plantain, unpeeled
175 g/6 oz jaggery (raw sugar; use brown sugar if jaggery is not available)

1 Cut the plantain into 5 cm/2 in lengths, put in a pan and add just enough water to cover.

2 Add the jaggery and cook for 35–40 minutes, until all the water has evaporated.

3 Allow to cool, peel, then chill and serve cold.

Below Plantain jaggery/kela gur

Cheese Fudge
(*Sandesh*)

Above Cheese fudge/Sandesh

Flat Bread Stuffed with Sweetened Lentils
(*Puran poori*)

SERVES 4
350 g/12 oz panir (see page 20), drained
75 g/3 oz sugar
1 tbsp pistachio nuts, finely chopped

1 Place the panir on a plate and rub with the palm of your hand until smooth and creamy.

2 Put the panir in a karai over medium heat, add the sugar and, stirring constantly, cook until it leaves the sides and a ball forms.

3 Remove from the heat and spread on a plate 1 cm/½ in thick. Cool slightly, sprinkle with the nuts and cut into small diamonds. Serve warm or hot.

SERVES 4
Filling
225 g/8 oz channa dal
about 750 ml/1¼ pt water
225 g/8 oz sugar
½ tsp ground cardamom
½ tsp saffron
Dough
225 g/8 oz wholewheat flour
1 tbsp oil
about 120 ml/4 fl oz hot water
ghee

1 To make the filling, wash the channa dal in several changes of water.

2 In a large saucepan, bring the dal and water to a boil over a medium high heat. Lower the heat, cover, leaving the lid slightly open, and simmer for about 1¼ hours until soft and thick. Remove from the heat.

3 Add the sugar, cardamom and saffron and stir well to mix thoroughly.

4 Return the pan to the heat and, stirring constantly, cook until thick and dry. Cool.

5 To make the dough, sieve the flour and rub in the oil.

6 Add enough water to make a stiff dough. Knead for about 8–10 minutes until soft and smooth.

7 Divide the dough into 10–12 balls.

8 Take a ball, flatten it on a slightly floured surface and roll into a round of 7.5 cm/3 in across. Place 1 tbsp of the filling in the centre and fold up the edges, enclosing the filling completely. Gently roll into a round 18 cm/7 across.

9 Place in a hot frying pan and cook over a medium heat for 1–2 minutes each side until brown spots appear.

10 Brush with melted ghee and serve hot.

Semolina Halva
(*Sooji halva*)

SERVES 4
3 tbsp ghee (see page 21)
25 g/1 oz almonds, blanched and
    sliced
100 g/4 oz semolina
1 tbsp raisins
400 ml/14 fl oz milk
65 g/2½ oz sugar

1 Heat the ghee in a karai over medium heat.

2 Add the almonds and fry for 1–2 minutes until golden brown. Remove with a slotted spoon and drain on a paper towel.

3 Put in the semolina and fry, stirring continuously, until golden. Add the raisins and mix with the semolina.

4 Add the milk and sugar and continue stirring until the mixture leaves the sides of the karai and a ball forms.

5 Serve on a flat dish garnished with the almonds.

Below Semolina halva/Sooji halva

Baked Yoghurt
(Payodhi)

SERVES 4
410 g/14½ oz can evaporated milk
397 g/14 oz can condensed milk
500 ml/18 fl oz yoghurt
1 tbsp pistachio nuts, skinned and
   chopped

1 Preheat the oven to 225°C/
450°F/Gas 5.

2 Whisk the evaporated milk,
condensed milk and yoghurt together for 1 minute.

3 Pour into an oven-proof dish and
place in the preheated oven.

4 Turn the oven off after 6 minutes
and leave the dish in the oven
overnight.

5 Chill. Serve garnished with the
chopped pistachio nuts.

Fritters in Syrup
(Malpoa)

SERVES 4
200 g/7 oz plain flour
1½ tsp baking powder
175 ml/6 fl oz yoghurt
approx 175 ml/6 fl oz milk
225 g/8 oz sugar
450 ml/16 fl oz water
oil for deep frying

1 Sieve together the flour and baking powder. Mix in the yoghurt.
Add enough milk to make a thick
batter.

2 Boil the sugar and water together for 10 minutes.

3 Heat the oil in a karai over medium high heat. Drop in 1 tbsp of the batter at a time and fry until crisp and brown. Drain on paper towels.

4 Soak the fried malpoa in the syrup for 5 minutes. Serve in a little syrup, hot or cold.

Below Fritters in syrup/Malpoa

Gujarati-style Creamed Rice
(Doodh pak)

SERVES 4
1.2 litres/2 pt milk
25 g/1 oz rice
40 g/1½ oz sugar
½ tsp ground cardamom
1 tbsp ground almonds

1 Bring the milk to a boil, stirring constantly.

2 Add the rice and sugar; stir to mix. Lower the heat, and, stirring occasionally, simmer until the milk has thickened and is reduced to about 500 ml/18 fl oz.

3 Remove from the heat and stir in the cardamom and almonds, making sure no lumps form when the nuts are added. Serve with hot Poori (see page 152).

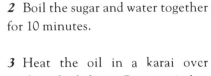

Yoghurt with Saffron
(*Shrikhand*)

SERVES 4

600 ml/1 pt yoghurt
1/4 tsp saffron
1 tbsp warm milk
100 g/4 oz caster sugar
2 tbsp pistachio nuts, skinned and
    chopped

1 Put the yoghurt in a muslin bag and hang it up for 4–5 hours to get rid of the excess water.

2 Soak the saffron in the milk for 30 minutes.

3 Whisk together the drained yoghurt, sugar and saffron milk till smooth and creamy.

Above Yoghurt with saffron/
Shrikhand

4 Put in a dish and garnish with the nuts. Chill until set.

(Any seasonal fruit may be added while whisking.)

Gram Flour Balls
(*Besan Laddu*)

SERVES 4

175 g/6 oz gram (chick pea) flour
6 tbsp ghee (see page 21)
100 g/4 oz sugar

1 Sieve the gram flour.

2 Heat the ghee in a heavy-based saucepan over a medium heat and fry the gram flour until golden.

3 Remove from the heat and cool. Add sugar and mix well.

4 When cold, make into small balls about the size of a walnut.

214

Cheese Balls in Syrup
(Rassogolla)

SERVES 4
300 g/11 oz panir (see page 20), drained
175 g/6 oz ricotta cheese
350 g/12 oz sugar
1.25 litres/2¼ pt water

1 Rub the panir and ricotta cheese with the palm of your hand until smooth and creamy. Divide into 16 balls.

2 Boil the sugar and water for 5 minutes over medium heat. Put the balls in the syrup and boil for 40 minutes.

3 Cover and continue to boil for another 30 minutes. Serve warm or cold.

Below Cheese balls in syrup/
Rassogolla

Khir with Oranges
(*Kamla khir*)

SERVES 4
1.2 litres/2 pt milk
40 g/1 ½ oz sugar
2 oranges, peeled

1 Boil the milk in a large sauce-pan, stirring constantly. Add the sugar and stir. Reduce heat and, stirring occasionally, simmer until it is reduced to 450 ml/¾ pt. Cool.

2 Remove all the pith from the oranges and slice. Add to the cooled milk. Serve chilled.

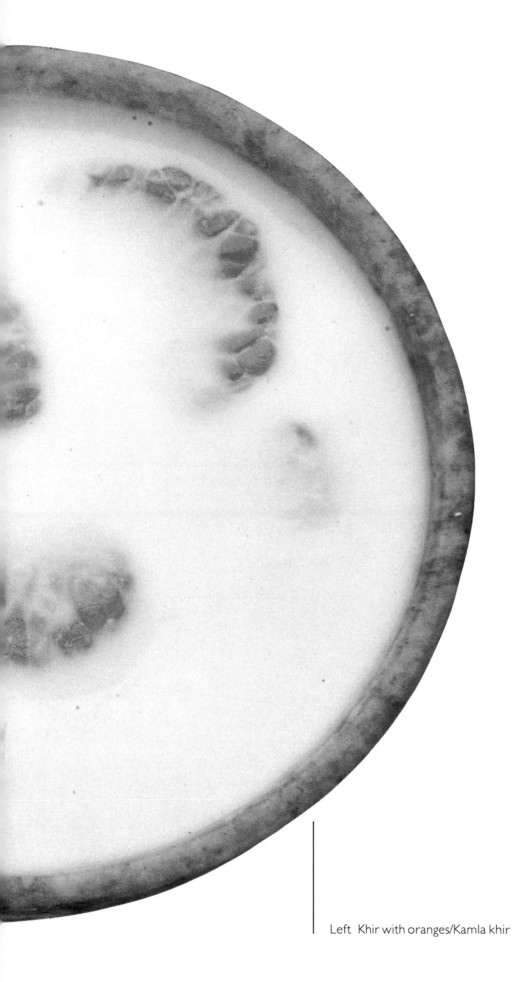

Left Khir with oranges/Kamla khir

Fried Sweets in Syrup
(Jelebi)

SERVES 4
150 g/5 oz plain flour
½ tsp baking powder
2 tbsp water
275 g/10 oz sugar
250 ml/8 fl oz water
few drops yellow food colouring
few drops rose water
oil for deep frying

1 Sieve together the flour and baking powder. Add enough milk to make a thick batter of pouring consistency. Keep aside in a warm place overnight.

2 When you are ready to fry the jelebis, prepare the syrup. Place the sugar and water in a large saucepan and bring to a boil. Boil for 5–6 minutes until it becomes slightly thick. Remove from the heat and add colouring and rose water. Stir well and keep aside.

3 Heat the oil over a medium high heat.

4 Place the batter in a piping bag with a 5 mm/¼ in plain nozzle. Squeeze the batter into the hot oil, making spiral shapes of about 6 cm/ 2½ in in diameter.

5 Fry until golden. Drain and add to the syrup for 1 minute. Remove from the syrup.

Carrot Halva
(Gajar halva)

Above Carrot halva/Gajar halva

Saffron Rice
(Zaffrani chawal)

SERVES 4
450 g/1 lb carrots, peeled and grated
900 ml/1 ½ pt milk
150 g/5 oz sugar
3 cardamoms
4 tbsp ghee (see page 21)
2 tbsp raisins
2 tbsp pistachio nuts, skinned and
    chopped

1 Place the carrots, milk, sugar and cardamoms in a large saucepan and bring to the boil. Lower the heat to medium low and, stirring occasionally, cook until all the liquid has evaporated.

2 Heat the ghee in a large frying pan over medium heat, add the cooked carrots, raisins and pistachios and, stirring constantly, fry for 15–20 minutes until the mixture is dry and reddish in colour. Serve hot or cold.

SERVES 4–6
275 g/10 oz basmati rice
½ tsp saffron
about 1 litre/1¾ pt boiling water
5 tbsp ghee (see page 21)
2–3 cardamom pods
50 g/2 oz almonds, slivered
65 g/2½ oz sugar
1 tbsp pistachio nuts, chopped

1 Wash the rice in several changes of water and soak in water for 15 minutes. Place the rice in a sieve to drain thoroughly.

2 Soak the saffron in 2 tbsp of the boiling water for 15 minutes.

3 Heat the ghee in a large saucepan over a medium high heat; add the cardamom and let it sizzle for 3–4 seconds. Add the drained rice and almonds and, stirring constantly, fry for 3–4 minutes until lightly golden.

4 Add the boiling water, saffron and sugar and stir to mix. Lower the heat to very low, cover and cook for about 20 minutes until all the water has been absorbed and the rice is tender.

5 Fluff with a fork, garnish with pistachio nuts and serve.

Rice Pudding
(*Chaler payesh*)

SERVES 4

1.2 litres/2 pt milk
1 tbsp basmati rice, washed
2 tbsp sugar
1 tbsp raisins
½ tsp ground cardamoms
1½ tbsp pistachio nuts, skinned and chopped

1 Bring the milk to the boil in a large pan, stirring continuously.

2 Lower the heat and simmer for 20 minutes. Add the rice and sugar and continue simmering for another 35–40 minutes until the milk has thickened and reduced to 600 ml/ 1 pt. During the cooking time stir occasionally to stop the milk sticking to the bottom of the pan.

3 Add the raisins and cardamoms and, stirring constantly, cook for a further 3–4 minutes.

4 Remove from the heat and garnish with the nuts. Serve hot or cold.

Right Rice pudding/ Chaler payesh

Glossary

Adrak Fresh ginger (see below).
Amchur Dried mango powder. Has a bittersweet flavour.
Amli Tamarind (see below).
Asafoetida A truffle-flavoured brown resin, available in powdered or lump form, and often used in cooking with beans. If you buy the lump form, crumble off a small piece and crush it between two sheets of paper.
Atta Wholewheat flour. Wheat is often ground at home in India and used to make unleavened flat breads.
Basmati rice The finest Indian long-grained rice, grown in the foothills of the Himalayas.
Besan Also known as gram flour, this is the flour made from chickpeas. It is used particularly in the south for making pancakes and steamed patties.
Biriyani A rice and vegetable, meat or seafood oven-cooked dish.
Cardamom Both black and green cardamoms are available, although the black ones are not often available. They are large and hairy. Use the green ones for the recipes in this book.
Channa dal A very versatile dried split pea. It looks like the ordinary yellow split pea, but is smaller with a sweeter, nuttier flavour. It can be cooked until soft for the dish called simply "dal", or, as in southern India, it can be used as a spice.
Chawal Rice.
Chick peas Also called gram or, in America, garbanzo beans. As chick peas often demand hours of cooking before they become tender, it is often cheaper to buy the tinned variety unless you have an old-fashioned kitchen range.
Chillies Can be bought fresh, in which case they are normally green, or dried, in which case they are red. Chillies are very hot and should be handled with care and used according to taste.
Cinnamon Can be bought powdered, or, better, in sticks. These sticks are the rolled bark of the cinnamon tree and have a warm spicy flavour.

Coconut Characteristic of the cooking of southern India. Buy a fresh coconut to extract the milk (see page 23) or use desiccated coconut to thicken sauces or garnish finished dishes. Desiccated coconut can be bought in most supermarkets and delicatessens.
Coriander Both the seeds and leaves of this plant are used. It can be grown as easily as parsley. The seeds are small and round, and are used either whole or ground. The leaves are bright green and have a strong bittersweet flavour.
Cumin seeds White or black, these seeds can be used whole or ground.
Curry leaves Can sometimes be bought fresh which is preferable to using them dried. Used extensively in the south of India, they are mainly added to food just before it is ready.
Dahi Yoghurt.
Dalchini Cinnamon (see above).
Dals Dried split peas, usually bought skinned.
Dhaniya Coriander (see above).
Elaichi Cardamom (see above).
Fenugreek seeds Chunky, tawny coloured seeds, often used roasted and ground. They have a bitter taste. Fenugreek leaves are a vegetable used like spinach, to which the plant is related.
Garam masala A mixture of spices ground together (see page 13), it is sprinkled on some dishes after they have been cooked.
Ghee Clarified butter. It can be made at home (see page 21) and does not need to be refrigerated.
Ginger Fresh ginger (*adrak*) is a fawn coloured rhizome. Ginger can also be bought powdered (*soondth*).
Gosht Meat. Goat is the meat most often eaten in India.
Gram flour Made from chick peas and also known as *besan*.
Haldi Turmeric (see below).
Halva A sweet dish.
Hara Green.
Hing Asafoetida (see above).

Jaggery Raw sugar, eaten as it is and used to flavour various dishes, even vegetable curries.
Jeera Cumin (see above).
Jingha Prawn or langoustine.
Kofta Meat or banana balls.
Kumban Mushroom.
Lassi A yoghurt drink (see page 21).
Luong Cloves.
Machi Fish.
Masala Spices.
Masoor dal Skinned split red lentils.
Moong dal Skinned split mung beans.
Murghi Chicken.
Mustard oil A yellow oil made from mustard seeds that is pungent when raw and sweet when heated. Much used in Kashmir and Bengal.
Mustard seeds Small yellow or black seeds often popped in hot oil, when they have a nutty sweet flavour. When ground for mustard powder their character is quite different – hot and smarting.
Narial Coconut (see above).
Neem Curry leaves (see above).
Papaya A fruit with good digestive properties.
Pilaf Fried rice dish.
Raita A cooling side dish made with yoghurt.
Roti Bread.
Sambar powder A southern Indian spice mix for vegetable curries (see page 15).
Soondth Powdered ginger (see above).
Tamarind The bean-like fruit of the tamarind tree, much used in southern Indian cooking.
Tava A flat cast-iron pan used for making bread.
Thali A large tray, often of wrought metal.
Toran A style of cooking where the dish remains dry.
Toovar dal A glossy dark yellow split pea.
Urid dal Polished split black lentils, often used as a spice in southern India.
Vark Silver and golf leaf used to decorate food on special occasions. It is edible.
Vindaloo A highly spiced and hot curry, traditionally from Goa.

Index